SOUTHAMPTON
THROUGH THE AGES

Erratum

The publisher draws your attention to the following:

The picture caption on page 140 wrongly refers to the view as being that of 'The High Street.'
It should be ' - A View Above Bar.'

SOUTHAMPTON
THROUGH THE AGES

PETER KILBY

Computational Mechanics Publications

Published by

Computational Mechanics Publications
Ashurst Lodge, Ashurst, Southampton SO40 7AA, UK
Tel: 44 (0)1703 293223; Fax: 44 (0)1703 292853
Email: wit@wessex.ac.uk
http://www.wessex.ac.uk

For USA, Canada and Mexico

Computational Mechanics Inc
25 Bridge Street, Billerica, MA 01821, USA
Tel: 508 667 5841; Fax: 508 667 7582
Email: cmina@ix.netcom.com

British Library Cataloguing-in-Publication Data

A Catalogue record for this book is available
from the British Library

ISBN: 1 85312 392 7 Computational Mechanics Publications, Southampton

Library of Congress Catalog Card Number 94-070469

The views expressed in this book are solely those of the author.

Printed and bound in Great Britain by Hobbs the Printers Limited, Southampton

Front cover illustration: Elizabethan Map. Reproduced by kind permission of the University of Southampton.
Back cover: Catchcold and Arundel Towers; Bugle Street; Reed Beds at Redbridge Causeway; The Non-Conformist Mortuary Chapel, Southampton Cemetery; Herbert Collins Estate and Carlton Crescent. Photographs by Peter Kilby.
Inside back cover: Peter Kilby. Photograph by Joe Low. Endpapers: *Reproduced by courtesy of Southampton Archive Services.*

ACKNOWLEDGEMENTS

I would like to give thanks to a number of people and organisations who have helped in many ways and given information to assist in the preparation of this book.

Firstly I wish to thank Councillor Margaret Singerman, Mayor of Southampton (1995-96), for graciously writing her foreword by way of an introduction. Next, my special thanks go out to Amanda Kilby, my daughter-in-law, who typed the original manuscript whilst deciphering some four hundred pages of hand written script. At the same time much of the photography, which gives the book its "eyes", owes itself to Joe Low, based at his Southampton studio, and full acknowledgement of each and every photograph is given elsewhere in these pages.

With reference to research for the book, much help and advice was received from the following: Sue Woolgar and her colleagues at the Southampton Archives Services; Similarly invaluable assistance came from Philip Preston and his colleagues at the Special Collections within the Hampshire County Library at the Civic Centre; University of Southampton, Hartley Library Special Collections; English Heritage, London; Countryside Education Trust, Beaulieu and the National Motor Museum, also at Beaulieu; Hampshire Wildlife Trust; Ordnance Survey, Southampton; Southern Daily Echo; Associated British Ports, Southampton; Cunard, Southampton and John Wiles at South Western House; British Airways; Lawrence Oxley Publishers, Alresford; BBC, Southampton.

And for help from individuals I have to thank: Mary Prendergast for her comments on Chapter 1; Jean Hudec for her comments on Chapter 2, Mrs Pat Arlott, wife of the late John Arlott, for permission to use his poem *By Night;* Professor Jeremy Hooker for permission to use his poem *At the Statue of Isaac Watts*; Richard Gilbert of Gilberts Bookshop for his loan of an 1833 edition of Rev. J. Silvester Davies' *A History of Southampton*. Richard Hunt of Highfields Estates for his loan of *Southampton Maps* published in 1964 by Southampton Corporation; Larry Wakefield for his invaluable information on the planning of the University of Southampton in the 1960s; Architects, Berry Webber and Partners for information on the designs of the Civic Centre; Architects, W.H. Saunders and Son for information on the Bargate Centre; Architects, Covell Matthews and Histon for information on Ocean Village; And last but not least I would like to thank my publisher Lance Sucharov and team at Computational Mechanics Publications, for their great help and encouragement; to Susannah Shores for her untiring work on graphics whilst updating the text and for the design of the cover, and finally to Professor Carlos Brebbia who asked me to write the book in the first place.

This book is dedicated
to all my family and to
the memory of my parents.

FOREWORD BY MARGARET SINGERMAN

MAYOR OF SOUTHAMPTON 1995-6

Southampton has a rich history stretching back through the ages. As a port its prosperity has flourished and waned on the strength of its foreign trade, except for a brief flirtation as a spa town in Regency times.

In spite of heavy damage during the Second World War many buildings of historic and architectural interest survive. Archaeology, including that of Roman and Saxon settlements, is closely documented as new developments take place.

Today's city is forward-looking and has international links, not only through its port and the new international terminal at Southampton Airport, but also through its University and Institute of Higher Education. Nevertheless, it jealously guards its heritage of buildings, parks and open spaces of which it is justly proud.

Margaret Singerman

CONTENTS

PROLOGUE

O for a booke and a shadie nook
Eyther in-a-doore or out;
With the grene leaves whispering overhede
Or the streete cryes all about.
Where I maie reade all at my ease,
Both of the newe and olde;
For a jollie good booke whereon to looke
Is better to me than golde.

John Wilson
19th century antiquarian book dealer

This book is essentially an overview of the development of Southampton as a city and port with a long history and priceless heritage. Its origins go back almost 2000 years when, in AD43, the Romans landed at *Clausentum* (Bitterne) on the east bank of the River Itchen, and stayed there for some 400 years, bringing with them an ordered and disciplined society from which grew civilisation and culture. After the departure of the Romans came the Anglo-Saxons from northern Europe. They were warriors at first but after colonisation turned to the peaceful pursuit of farming, founding the township of Saxon *Hamwic* on the west bank of the River Itchen in the 8th century AD. Following Viking incursions and other economic circumstances, the inhabitants of Hamwic moved westwards to the site of the present day medieval walled town. This natural defensive escarpment was lapped by the waters of the River Test to the west of the old Town Walls, the origins of which date back to the 11th century and the Norman Conquest. The walled town passed through many vicissitudes of fortune until Elizabethan times

MADONNA FIGURE FROM ST. DENYS CHURCH

when, at the end of the 16th century, a decline set in which was only to be revived in the early 18th century by the discovery of natural springs and the bracing effects of sea bathing. This led to the so-called Spa and Resort periods in the town's history, bringing a new affluence by the influx of the 'Gentlemen's Party' and associated wealth.

In the 19th and 20th centuries there were to be dramatic changes to the topography of the town, brought about by large scale land reclamation of the mudflats. Thus, the old docks were created in the 19th century and the new docks in the 20th century, and the Port of Southampton was formed which, blessed with dual tides, would assist well with shipping movements for both commercial and passenger vessels.

Throughout the ebb and flow of people and traffic, ideas have similarly been exchanged, and we see in the buildings of this cosmopolitan city a wealth of design ideas left as a legacy from the past, notwithstanding the ravages of the Second World War air raids.

History has been enacted here, people have both prospered and perished, and the town has known plenty and want. The single thread which runs throughout its history is the seemingly natural trend towards expansion and rejuvenation, extolling the virtues of the sea and the splendid site on which Southampton stands. With water on three of its sides and beautiful open spaces, the town is exampled by its two rivers and sequential areas of parks and other green spaces which act like lungs to its inner body.

Southampton has produced its fair share of famous people who either were born or achieved fame here. King Canute in the 11th century is remembered for his admonishment of his fawning courtiers by not holding back the waters of the sea. Tradition has it that Henry V in 1415 addressed his troops outside the Bargate before embarking for the Battle of Agincourt, and dispatched the perpetrators of the famous conspiracy against him. John Carver led forth the Pilgrim Fathers in 1620 to found America, and early this century in 1912 another set of voyagers left for America on the maiden and last voyage of the ill-fated *Titanic*. Isaac Watts wrote the hymn 'Our God our Help in Ages Past' from his house in French Street, the music of which is commemorated by the peal of bells in the Civic Centre tower, playing the tune which reminds us of our long heritage. R.J. Mitchell, who designed the Spitfire before his death in 1937, and lived in a modest house in Russell Place in Portswood, was responsible for the production of a day and night fighter in Southampton's Supermarine Works which, for its time, was the most lethal fighting machine ever invented and for which it seems the city suffered a dreadful retribution in the air raids of the 1940s. As a result of the destruction which followed, and in the aftermath of the Second World War, a vast reconstruction programme ensued, and with its progress through the much maligned 1960s (architecturally speaking) the city is again poised on a new era of development, which together with all necessary care and attention to its historic fabric, will change its face again, leading us into the 21st century.

PETER KILBY

EXTRACT FROM MAP OF ROMAN ENGLAND
Showing the strategic location of Clausentum in relation to London and key towns on the south coast.
(Reproduced by courtesy of the Ordnance Survey.)

1. HISTORICAL INTRODUCTION

THE ROMAN PERIOD

Southampton has been a port for almost 2000 years, since AD43 when Roman ships (galleys) landed at *Clausentum*, now the site of Bitterne Manor, and soldiers set up camp there, on a peninsula of land on the River Itchen bounded on three sides by tidal waters, and defended on the landward by two parallel *fossae* or ditches. From this strategic position in central Southern England would radiate the system of Roman roads as set out in the *Antonine Itinerary* (compiled in AD320), linking Clausentum with *Venta Belgarum* (Winchester) to the north, and *Portus Adurni* (Portchester) to the east. The whole of this Roman road system was built during the 400 years or so of the Roman occupation, when a network of roads was extended over the entire country, including Wales and parts of the lowlands of Scotland beyond Hadrian's Wall in the north of England.

These roads were a remarkable feat of engineering, built in unremitting straight lines from minor to major settlements, lesser walled towns to cantonal capitals, being paved in stone and built above the general level of the terrain (hence the origin of 'High Street'). Each section of road was marked in Roman miles, i.e. *Milia Passuum*, being a thousand paces and each pace or *passus* being made up of two steps both left and right. Thus it was that Clausentum was X (ten) Roman miles from Venta Belgarum, and X (ten) Roman miles from Portus Adurni. A Roman mile is roughly equivalent to 1620 yards (1481 metres), and is therefore smaller than the modern mile of 1760 yards (1609 metres).

The scene was therefore set by the Roman landing at Clausentum for the future development of Southampton, both as a port and a point of entry into central Southern England. Geographically, Southampton today occupies a site between

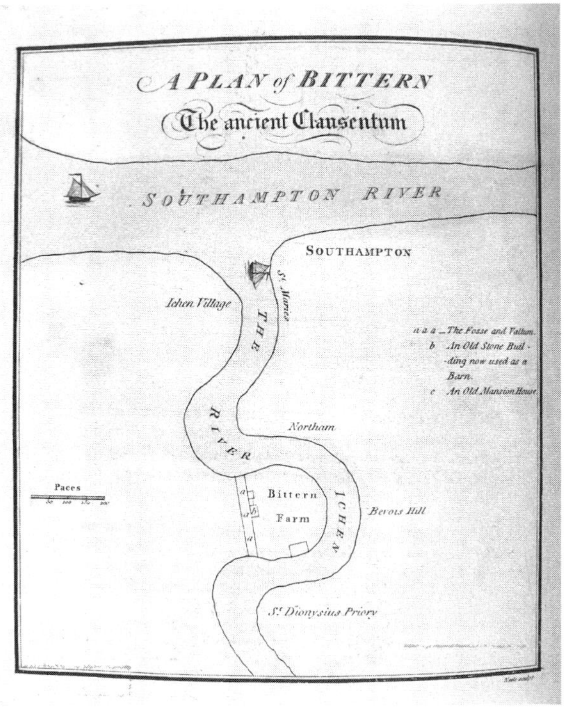

PLAN OF CLAUSENTUM
Map by the Rev. Richard Warner in 1792.
Reproduced by courtesy of Hampshire County Library Southampton Special Collections.

the confluence of two rivers, i.e. the River Itchen to the east and the River Test to the west, dicharging as they do into Southampton Water and the Solent beyond. The port of Southampton is notable for its dual tides, giving high water twice a day, a fact noted by the Venerable Bede, who in the 8th century wrote: 'in this narrow sea the two tides of the ocean ... daily meeet and oppose one another beyond the north of the River Homlea [Hamble]'.

This phenomenon was elaborated upon by Philip Brannon who, in 1850 wrote: 'the tides here present can fortunately be numbered among the many circumstances favourable to Southampton. After reaching high-water mark, the tide ebbs an hour, then flows again for one hour, thus reaching high-water mark a second time, or in other words, giving an actual duration of nearly four hours full tide.'

Strategically the site of Clausentum was well chosen by the Romans, set into the mouth of the River Itchen on a sharp bend, affording scope for all round visibility, thereby diminishing the probability of surprise by an enemy. The name Clausentum implies these qualities of defence, being derived, according to John Duthy, from the Latin *clausus*, shut up, and *intus*, within. No obvious evidence exists today of this Roman occupation, apart from the remains of the Bath House and a small section of wall, the site having been bisected by the road leading to the Northam Bridge and heavy development all around. Happily, however, the site of Bitterne Manor on the foreshore with its remaining spacious grounds, affords the opportunity of contemplating the character of the site of the Roman camp, although we must look to writers from the past for a description of the remains of the fortifications. In 1883 the Reverend J. Silvester Davies published *A History of Southampton*, based on papers previously produced by a Dr John Speed, who is quoted as saying of Clausentum: 'on the inner bank of this (most western or inner) ditch, towards the north end of it is still standing an old stone building now converted into a barn, but which appears to me to have been part of an old Roman fort, for in the upper part of the wall next to the ditch are slits to shoot arrows through'. He goes on to say: 'At the north end of the barn are still to be seen some remains of the foundations of the old walls of the fort, about four feet in thickness'.

John Duthy writing earlier in 1839 states: 'Clausentum consisted of the station, surrounded by a wall, principally

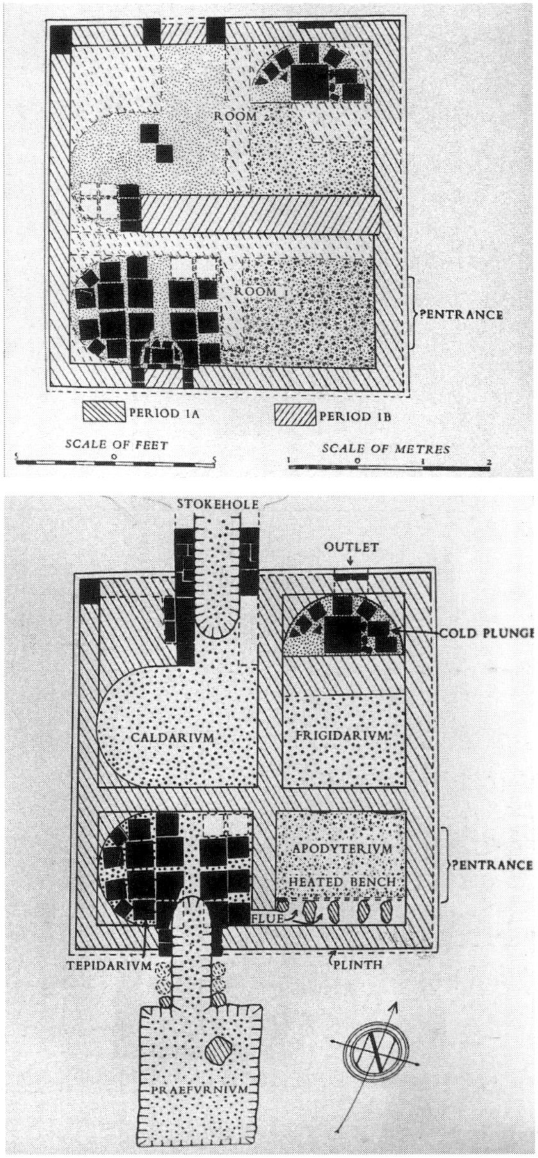

BATH HOUSE
Excavations carried out in 1951 by Cotton and Gathercole revealed this small private Bath House dated circa ad170-180. (Reproduced by courtesy of English Heritage.)

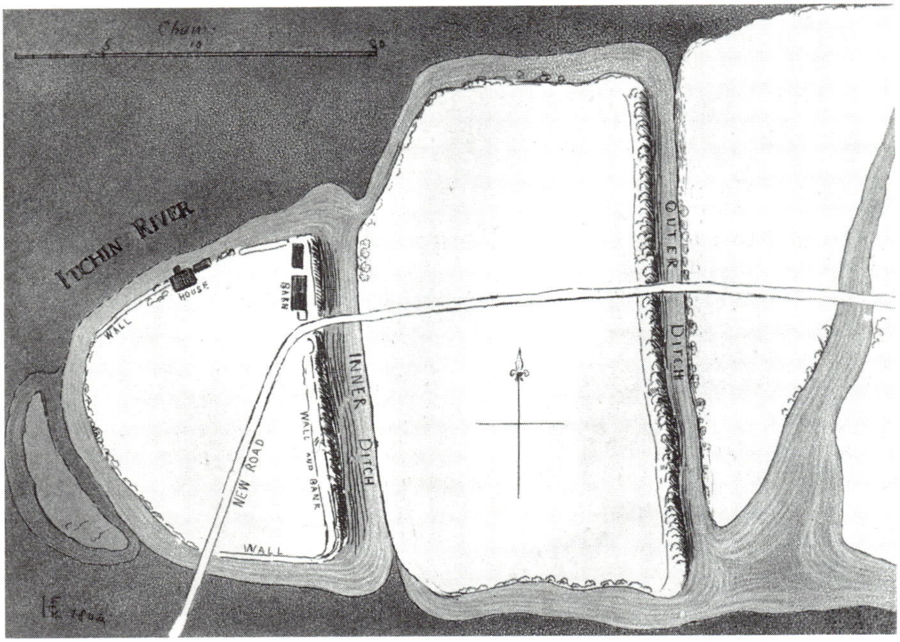

ROMAN STATION
This hand drawn map by Sir H.C. Englefield in 1841 illustrates the main features of the layout of Clausentum, protected by water to the north, west and south and to the east by two large ditches with stockades.
Reproduced by courtesy of Hampshire County Library Southampton Special Collections.

built of flint, faced very roughly with small square stones, and having a bonding course of large flat bricks running through its interior part. Of these bricks, fragments may yet be seen on the shore of the field, lying to the eastward of the Portsmouth and Southampton Road. The wall had no foundation whatsoever, but was literally set down on the surface of the ground; and much of it has consequently, in the process of time, been undermined by the flood of the Itchen'. Reference this time is made to a wall nine feet (2.74m) thick (as opposed to four (1.21m)) obviously the nature of the fortifications varied throughout its length. It is interesting to note that John Duthy's description extends to the position of the remains of the ditch, which at that time 'may be clearly seen' in the vicinity of a 'small public house called the Bridge Tavern'.

It is always difficult in history to decide where facts end and supposition begins, but it is clear that Clausentum was an important settlement, defending as it did the approach to Winchester to the north and the route southwards to the Isle of Wight, and at the same time providing a safe haven for galleys coming to this country from France and beyond. Clausentum's position was also important in connection with the Roman road systems leading inland from this point of entry (and elsewhere). The routes of an estimated 6000 miles of Roman roads can be seen in many places today. It is along these roads that the Roman legions advanced, bringing civilisation and security to the country's inhabitants for almost 400 years until the year AD406 when Constantine III finally withdrew his troops from Britain to undertake the conquest of Gaul and Spain. The erosion of the numbers of Roman troops in Britain had taken place over a period of time to deal with troubles elsewhere. The construction of Hadrian's Wall in the north of England was significant in that it marked the first evidence of containment of the Roman Empire, being both a physical barrier and a symbol of the decline which was to follow.

THE SAXON PERIOD

Unlike Clausentum the Saxon town of *Hamwic,* situated on the west bank of the River Itchen estuary, was not a fortified town (notwithstanding evidence of a western defensive ditch). It was in essence an important local trading settlement and international trading port. It has been described as being 'one of the largest towns in England, comparable with London, Canterbury and York'. Much archaeological evidence exists today concerning the area now occupied by St Mary's Church and Six Dials. Originally this pear-shaped town was situated adjacent to a lagoon on the banks of the Itchen, the riverline of which has changed over the centuries; its original shape is shown in the Elizabethan map of Southampton. The natural reclamation process of the lagoon into salt marshes and then into land had occurred by the time Mazell's map of 1771 was published.

Modern evidence would suggest that Hamwic (the forerunner of Southampton) was founded in AD688-726 by King Ine. John Duthy says of the Saxon origins of the city that plans were in progress for building a church there 'and from that

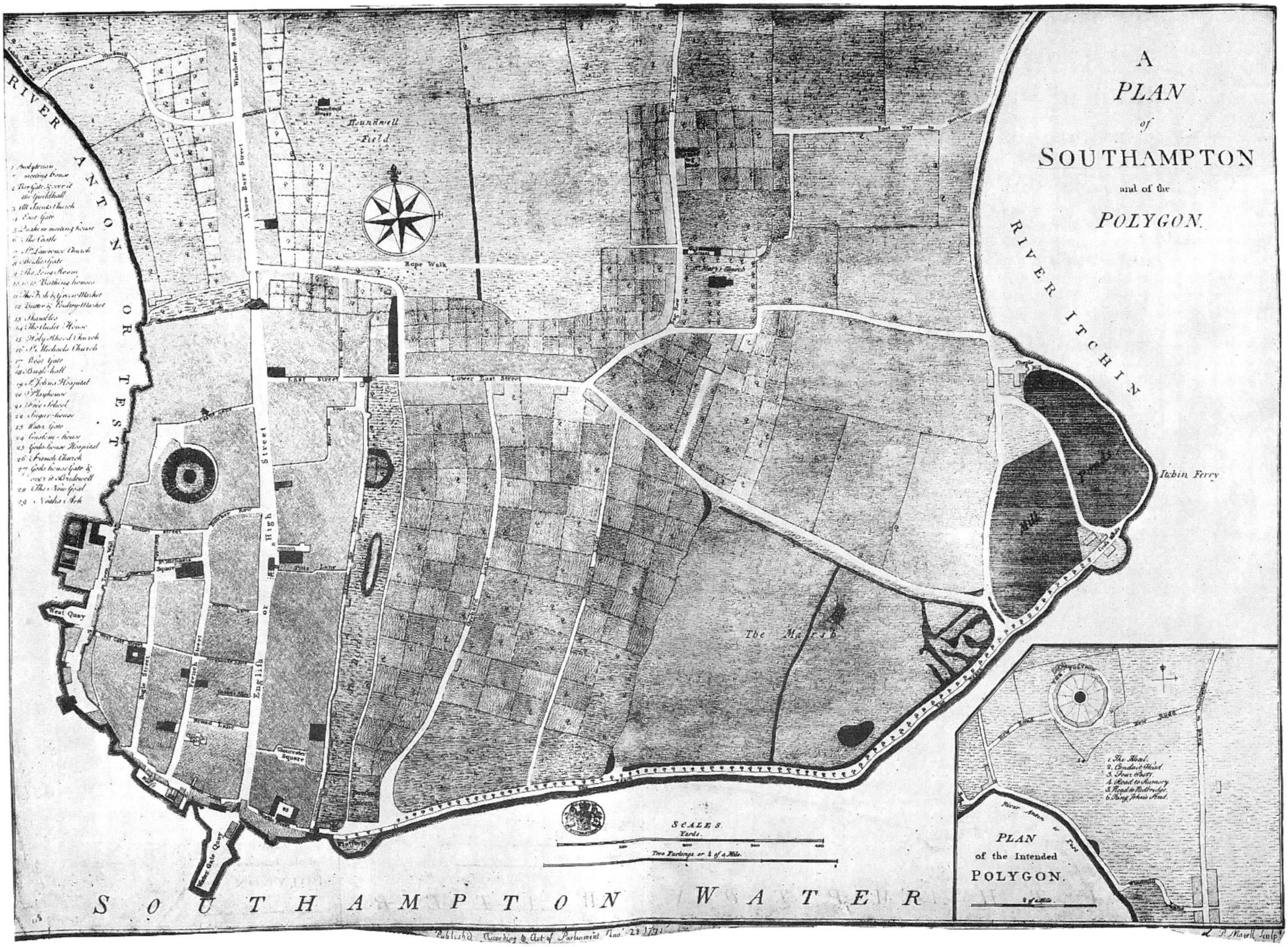

MAZELL'S MAP OF 1771
This map shows the location of the site of Hamwic situated around St Mary's Church and its relationship with the River Itchen, now without the lagoon of Saxon times which apparently silted up over the centuries to form marshes and changes in topography.
Reproduced by courtesy of Southampton Archive Services.

period it rapidly increased until it became one of the first cities in the Kingdom'. Interestingly, the mention of a church in Hamwic relates to the earlier introduction of Christianity into Saxon England, when in AD597 St Augustine, Pope Gregory's representative from Rome, landed on the Isle of Thanet in north-east Kent. From there he sent forth forty Christian monks to convert the natives, having first convinced Ethelbert, King of Kent by preaching to the assembled court. According to the Venerable Bede, King Ethelbert received Augustine by saying: 'your words and promises are fair indeed, but they are new and uncertain and I cannot accept them and abandon the age old beliefs of the whole English nation. But since you have travelled far ... we shall not harm you. Nor will we forbid you to preach and convert.'

The introduction of Christianity into this country was to have a profound effect on the architecture of the religious foundations which were to follow - and St Mary's Church therefore will have been the first of such 'permanent' buildings to have been located later on the site of Anglo-Saxon Southampton ('that minster of Hamwic' mentioned in 1045 in a South Stoneham Charter).

Reference has already been made to the likely foundation dates for Hamwic (i.e. between AD688-726). Of this Alan Morton explains in *Excavations at Hamwic*: 'in its different guises as Hamwic and Hamtun, the place was, or possessed, a mercimonium in AD721, headed a shire of some sort in AD757, was one of a number of important towns burned in AD764, and was threatened by the Vikings in AD840 and in the same year was possessed of a royal villa'.

Hamwic had thus grown up on the opposing bank of the River Itchen to Clausentum, and so commenced the east to west movement of the epicentre of Southampton, culminating in the siting of the medieval walled town on the estuary of the River Test. This westward movement has continued into modern times with the land reclamations, forming the old docks in the early 19th century and the new docks in the early 20th century.

David Lloyd, writing in the Hampshire volume of the *Pevsner Buildings of England* says: 'St Mary's the Mother Church of Southampton descended from the original church of Saxon Hamwic, and sited on what was the rural fringe of the town in the early middle ages'. This alludes to the Saxon economy based on the rewards of agriculture. The south of England was originally forested, but timber being the prime source of fuel and the material for building resulted in the gradual clearance of these forests for agricultural purposes, namely the growing of crops and the rearing of animals. Emperor Constantine, writing in the year AD310 had already anticipated this development when he wrote: 'How lucky you are Britain, more blessed than any other land, endowed by nature with every benefit of soil and climate'.

Thus in the early Anglo-Saxon period, with the passing of the Roman occupation and part of their road system presumably still in place, Hamwic must have prospered as a point of distribution for the export of raw materials, of which wool was the most important, and the import of manufactured commodities. Around the town however,

HAMWIC - Southampton's Saxon Town. An artist's impression of Six Dials site at about AD750. Note the gravelled main street and side streets leading off to the houses which were mainly single storey with mud or wattle and daub walls and straw roofs. Reproduced by courtesy of Southampton City Museums.

the farming community lived in scattered villages and farms, in houses built from walls of timber framing (with wattle and daub) or cob (i.e. mud/chalk and straw), and with straw roofs. The same house construction would have applied to towns such as Hamwic, and archaeological evidence supports this supposition.

The extent of the boundaries of Hamwic are difficult to establish, and estimates vary from 17-45 hectares, with a variable within these areas for estimating the population figures. The streets within the town were straight and about five metres wide, and planned on a north-south east-west grid. The surfaces of these roads were metalled with gravelled surfaces, suggesting a planned layout and orderly society. Importantly also, evidence exists of a system of water supply by wells and arrangements for sewage disposal via cesspits. The houses were probably single storey with hearths for warmth, and some of the buildings were thought to have an 'industrial' use, as witnessed by the results of archaeological excavations.

Hamwic was abandoned in the late 9th century and its remains lay undisturbed until, in the late 18th century, work began on the Southampton to Salisbury canal, which revealed in one section of its cuttings the pre-existence of this pre-medieval town. It was not until the 1980s, however, that full-scale excavations revealed the extent and history of this settlement and its population, assessed as between 8,000 and 10,000 in its heyday, (although estimates of this figure vary to as low as 2,000 in the settlement's decline).

Be that as it may, the excavations revealed, from the 200 or so burials found on the site, (east to west in Christian fashion), the following evidence of the people who lived there: the Anglo-Saxons were a sturdy race of 5'7" (1.7m) average height, with blue eyes and fair hair, with a life expectancy of about 30-40 years. These people were not hunters. Their food supplies were sustained by a well-established rural base, which provided, in addition to arable products, meat from cattle, sheep and pigs, and fish caught locally (in the Southampton Water), comprising eels, plaice and flounder. An industrial base has already been referred to, and this in the main was what is called a 'bone industry', in other words using bones from slaughtered animals to make, for example, spindle whorls, needles and weaving instruments. Leading on from this, other activities included weaving on looms, textile and leather production, and even the art of gilding, effected by mixing gold and mercury in a bowl.

Pottery found on site was made from a local clay called brick earth, and led to the production of utilitarian objects used for cooking and storage. There were also links with pottery originally in the New Forest, and there is evidence of a North Sea and Channel trading pattern linking Hamwic with La Londe near Rouen in France, for example.

Coins discovered provide evidence of an elementary money trading system, as opposed to bartering. These small silver coins called *sceattas* were replaced by pennies of silver which carried the name of the king and moneyer, during the reign of King Offa (AD757-96).

In spite of all this orderly, well-regulated and, for its time, relatively sophisticated, society, Hamwic as a port and trading centre declined and depopulation of this centre of affluence began around AD850. This was brought about by the general economic depression affecting northern Europe at that time, because of the ever increasing activities of the Vikings. As a result Hamwic was gradually closed down and the population withdrew westwards to the safer haven of what was to become the medieval walled and fortified town, situated on an escarpment facing the estuary of the River Test.

CLAUSENTUM AND HAMWIC TODAY

CLAUSENTUM

The layout of Clausentum, when superimposed on a relatively modern Ordnance Survey map on which the river boundaries of 1820 are noted, reveals the

BATH HOUSE FOUNDATIONS
These are the exciting remains of a sophisticated civilization which bear witness to an ordered and technologically advanced society.

THE DEFENSIVE 'FOSSE'
It is difficult to imagine the full impact of these earthwork defences now the fosse or ditch is overgrown, although in its day it was full of serious intent. The fosse provided landward protection for Clausentum, with additional defence provided by wooden stakes driven into the ground alongside (like the ditch in the later medieval walled town, this fosse would have filled with water to complete its protective influence).

approximate boundaries of the site and location of the outer bank and ditch to the west of Rampart Road, and the inner fosse and stockade to the west of Bitterne Manor. Archaeological excavations carried out in the 1950s by the Ancient Monuments Inspectorate of the then Ministry of Works revealed and traced the line of the inner ditch or fosse in which 100 stake holes were unearthed, 'cut in the natural gravel, six or seven inches in diameter'. These additional wooden defences were thought to have originated from the 4th century to provide additional defence from Saxon sea raiders. At the same time, the foundations of an almost square stone building dating from AD170 were found. This would have been a bath house comprising an *apodyterium* or changing room, a *tepidarium* (cool room), a *caldarium* (hot bath), and a *frigidarium* or cold bath.

Retracing the history of the site again, in the 12th and 13th centuries a substantial manor house was built. This building was essentially the centrepiece of a large farm which remained so through to the 19th century, when an enlarged Victorian country mansion was built. (A window from this house is preserved in the Gods House Tower Archaeology Museum in Winkle Street, in which there is a glass engraving of the building itself.) In 1899 most of the grounds were sold for suburban development and the mansion stood as an ivy-clad ruin for many years. In 1948 however, the renowned Southampton architect Herbert Collins drew up plans for its restoration and conversion into flats, while restoring the ruins which remained. This building today is known as Bitterne Manor and is scheduled as a Grade II Listed Building.

Through its 2000 years of history, attempts have been made to unravel the mysteries of Clausentum. The Reverend R. Warner writing in 1792 best sums up the problem when he says: 'it is a mortifying consideration to the pride of man, that his most magnificent and elaborate works which either vanity dictates, or utility enjoins, have all their determined periods of decay, beyond which their duration cannot be extended'!

BITTERNE MANOR TODAY
Restoration and conversion of the stone ruins into flats was carried out by Herbert Collins in 1948.

BY NIGHT

The South-west wind goes down before the night
And soundlessly the river southers by:
The crumbling walls are chalked in moonbeam-white
On trees pinned out with stars across the sky.
A still and sharply-lined grey figure fills
The glassless window of a floorless room,
And creeper on a smashed door-pillar spills
Across the hallway's shuttered trap of gloom.
Now with the mask of midnight on its face,
The faithful river mutely toils to force
The bank that bars the long dry fosse and race
Once more along the old remembered course,
To make again the old full-circle sweep
And, with its body, guard Clausentum's sleep.

SONNET BY JOHN ARLOTT 1946
Written in the grounds of Bitterne Manor. This is a moving description, not only of Clausentum when Bitterne Manor stood empty, but it also alludes to the long history of the site. The opening line refers to the "South-West wind"; Southampton's trademark.
Reproduced by kind permission of the trustees of John Arlott, deceased.

HAMWIC

As previously stated, the exact boundaries of the Anglo-Saxon town are not easy to establish with certainty, only the general shape. One thing is certain, however, the site now occupied by St Mary's Church was part of the township, and around the present building the origins of previous Christian churches and burials can be traced. The present church was built in 1878-84 to the designs of E.G. Street, on the site of a major collegiate church of the Middle Ages. It was almost totally destroyed in the Second World War (only the lower walls of the nave and tower with spire remained) and was again rebuilt in 1954-6. Externally the building makes a splendid composition and landmark, while internally some fine stained glass (which survives from 1880) by Clayton and Bell is seen in the baptistry. The church is surrounded by a huge church-yard, which together with its mature trees and grassed areas, assumes today the semblance of a small inner city park.

ST MARY'S CHURCH
This marks the centre of Christian Hamwic; several previous churches have been built on the same site. Photograph by Peter Kilby.

2. THE MEDIEVAL WALLED TOWN AND TOWN QUAYS

INTRODUCTION

When King Harold died, shot in the eye at the Battle of Hastings in 1066, it marked the end of the Anglo-Saxon era and the beginning of the influences of the Norman Conquest in Britain. The victorious King William I (1066-1087), named 'the Conqueror', set about subjugating the land and in 1086 ordered the so-called 'Domesday Survey'. This survey was a meticulous account of the details of ownership and wealth, and also presents a fascinating social commentary of the times some 900 years ago.

The general area of Southampton is covered by what is called the 'Mansbridge Hundred' and refers in part to the districts of Southampton, Millbrook, Redbridge, Shirley, Woolston and South Stoneham (as well as North Stoneham, now outside the city boundary). For instance it says of Millbrook 'it was always in the (lands of the) Monastery. Before 1066 and now it answered for 5 hides. The villagers held and hold it. There is no hall. Land for 5 ploughs. 28 villagers with 5 ploughs. Meadow, 14 acres; woodland at 5 pigs. Value before 1066, later, and now 100s'. And so it was that this avaricious King held sway and controlled the people of this land by extracting taxes and dues.

1066 marked the beginnings of the Medieval Period in English architecture, with the introduction of the robust and solid Romanesque style called *Norman*. Its distinctive stone semi-circular arched doors, windows and arcading could be found in both military and ecclesiastical architecture. The Norman influence is now seen in the old medieval town of Southampton, in churches like St Julian's Chapel in Winkle Street and St Michael's Church in St Michael's Square. This Norman style

SHIELDS
There are eleven on the north face of the Bargate (Two in the spandrels of the archway and nine in the frieze) to include the crosses of both St George for England and St Andrew for Scotland.

with its strange new ornamentation, most characteristically *chevron*, i.e. zigzag in form, was a distinct departure from the simplicity of Saxon architecture, which still survives at the Church of St Lawrence, Bradford-on-Avon, or the Church of St Mary at Breamore in Hampshire. In Saxon buildings spaces were spanned between walls and columns using inclined beams – a relatively unsophisticated form of construction called 'trabieated' (i.e. post and beam). In Norman architecture however, a new dimension in structural arrangement was introduced by the use of both groined and ribbed vaulting, to span in stone three-dimensional roof spaces mainly in churches. Ribbed vaulting, i.e. the use of stone ribs and infill diaphragms of brick or stone, is epitomised *par excellence* in the nave of Durham Cathedral.

So it was that a significant new style in architectural design and construction had been introduced into this country from the continent, and so it was also that Southampton, facing as it does towards the estuary of the River Seine in France, was poised to become an important instrument both as a port in Norman times and as a centre for architectural innovation.

Without doubt the most important building in the town walls of medieval Southampton is the Bargate, or *Barr Gate* as it was once called, situated to the north of the old town in line with Above Bar Street to the north and High Street to the south, forming part of a sequence of stone built fortifications. The Bargate itself would appear to be the earliest of the fortifications, its construction having begun in about 1180-1200, and is described by Pevsner Lloyd as 'probably the finest, and certainly the most complex, town gateway in Britain'. As for the town walls, those sections remaining rank third only to say York and Chester in their extent and completeness. These majestic walls, once continuous, stretched overall to about one and a quarter miles and contained some 29 towers and seven gates. They are unique in being part of an English medieval fortified *sea* town.

Walking from the Bargate westwards, i.e. anti-clockwise, the walls commence and extend to Arundel Tower (linked across Castle Way by a modern bridge connecting the upper walkways) and from thence stretch southwards along the Western Esplanade, with a sheer drop of over 20 feet (6.09 metres) from the ramparts in Forest View to the road below. The walls continue along with extensive arcading, almost unbroken until the site of Bugle Tower is reached, just north of the Mayflower Memorial. Within this section we pass Catchcold Tower (15th century with three gunports, and the earliest in Europe), the forty stone steps adjacent having been added in 1850, the Castle Watergate and Castle Vault (for storing the King's wine) and the site of the castle itself behind. Further south is the William Nicholl's Tower, close to the Royal Standard Public House, built into the walls themselves, and leading on to the mid 14th century West Gate, the prime importance of which was that it led directly on to West Quay. Beyond this we see the further spectacular stone arcading, five arches in all, with just the hint of a pointed arch. Seen at a distance they look almost semi-circular, while in the walls behind the arches window openings from previous houses are visible. Beyond this point the walls tail away, and there is an open space in which one can see the Mayflower Memorial. Here the walls forming the sea defences of the past end, and only remain in fragments until Gods House Tower and gate is reached at the south-east corner of the town. The walls move northwards again until they arrive at Polymond Tower

WESTERN ESPLANADE
This panoramic view of the town walls to the west bears witness to their completeness and powerful presence. Photograph by Peter Kilby.

and then turn west towards the Bargate once more.

It would be as well to pause here and retrace our steps to where the seas once lapped against the walls on the Western Esplanade, and to consider the function and history of West Quay.

Looking again at the 1771 map, it can be seen that this quay was approached through the arch of West Gate and, like the Bargate, was the space through which commerce and armies passed, to and from the continent and elsewhere. To the north, a minor quay serviced Southampton Castle for the King. With reference to the castle, little now remains, apart from some evidence of foundations immediately behind the wall adjacent to Castle Square, and an arcade of stone walling near the junction of Castle Way and Albion Place, next to the present Masonic Hall. The castle itself is recorded as being in ruins in the year 1635 while a hundred years before, Leland writing at that time describes the castle as 'both larg, fair and very strong'. Dr. Speed writing in 1770 says 'the Castle was no part of the fortifications in which the town was concern'd but always belonged to the King. The site of it was granted away by King Charles I to one George Gollop Esq.' He goes on to say 'it is not easy to determine the precise time when the town ceas'd to be a garrison, but its consequence in that respect grew daily less, in proportion to the increase of Portsmouth, and I do not apprehend that it was ever considered in that light after the Restoration'.

It is interesting to note in respect of Dr Speed's accounts that Mazell's map, published at about the same time as his writings, gives a clear indication of the layout of both the medieval (and Saxon) town sites, together with the suburb environs. Note the delineation of West Quay opposite Westgate Street, and the West Gate which figures greatly in Southampton's history. The completeness of the Town Wall at that time is seen on the map, although while confirming the facts Dr Speed says 'the walls are still standing around the town, but are in a ruinous condition, only those on the south and west side which are close to the sea, are kept in such repair and to prevent damage from the sea'. So things stood at that date, following the evolution of these majestic defences from the early 13th century onwards, until the final completion and strengthening of the sea-facing sides following the ravages of the 1338 French raid and eventual decline.

The construction of these town defences is central to the theorising by historians as to when the medieval walled town superseded the Saxon settlements of Hamwic (and the later Saxon site within the current curtain wall). The impetus for this new town site came into being with the Norman Conquest, together with the need to accommodate and defend the new continental link with France. Two distinct communities needed to be housed, namely the English in the All Saints, Holy Rood and St Lawrence parishes, while the French settled in the parishes of St Michael and St John. The Domesday Survey of 1086 records 'in the Borough of Southampton the King has in lordship 76 men who pay £7 of land tribute'. Reference is also made to those who 'have the customary dues of their houses in Southampton by grant of King William'. In other words, in the late 11th century a township nucleus, at least, existed here and so continued the east to west movement of the epicentre of the town.

The layout of the town within the walls to which we have referred is of considerable interest. The spinal cord is without doubt the slightly off-centre and south to north axis of the High Street (or English Street as it was called), linking through to the Bargate and Above Bar to the north and Water Gate Quay to the south. Between this road, the western defences and the line of the sea we see French Street and Bugle Street, again north-south in orientation, with east-west roads Castle Lane to the north, Butcher Row and Simnel Street in the centre, and West Gate Street and Brewhouse Lane to the south (to name but some of the principal roads). Beyond the Town Wall to the west and south are the quay facilities, and to the east the Town Ditch. The street pattern is generally laid out on a grid, and therefore has every sign of a planned configuration. It is from this core that the town expanded outwards to the north and east and in its eastward expansion overgrew St Mary's and Bitterne, from which its origins began.

BARGATE (North Side)
'The Gateway to England' and to 'one of the neatest and completest towns'

EVOLUTION AND EXPANSION

THE BARGATE

The **Bargate** is, as previously stated, the most important of not only the existing buildings but also of those lost to posterity, within the walls enclosing the medieval town. It forms what has been traditionally called the 'Gateway to England'. As a building it is an amalgamation of styles and characteristics, combining a dark and once grime-encrusted north front, which encloses the original Norman circular tower, with a central archway flanked by two leaden lions in sentinel attitudes. Above the facade is punctuated by the central cruciform loophole and the sparkle of brightly emblazoned shields. A visitor to this place wrote in 1635 'Hence [from Winchester] away then I hastened to one of the neatest and completest towns in all these western parts, into which I had entered at the Northgate [Bargate] there of with no little fear, between the jaws of 2 ramping lions and 2 thundering warriors Exipat, that fearful giant on one side, and brave Bevis of Southampton on the other, if above them had not been placed our late renowned virtuous Q. Elizabeth, to

SENTINEL LIONS
These lions, cast in lead in 1743, were originally carved from wood and are so mentioned in the Court Leet book of 1619 where there is an order for their being varnished.

daunt their courage and quell their fury, and to suffer peaceable passengers to have safe and quiet entrance'. (This passage makes reference to the legendary Sir Bevis (or Bevois) and his giant, Squire Ascupart, whose figures then appeared on painted panels, mentioned by Pepys when he visited the town in 1662, and now removed to the guildhall above). The date and description, i.e. '1635', and 'completest town', makes interesting reading and serves as one source of confirmation of the Bargate's part in the town's development, notwithstanding Dr Speed's later description of the state of the castle building as 'an old ruinated castle'.

In contrast to the north side, the south side of the Bargate is constructed in a completely different style, with a flat, clean, stone facade. At first floor level, stone traceried windows in the decorated gothic style of the 14th century can be seen; now inside the town's defences, the Bargate looks less like a fortification, although there are still pointed stone arches below and masonry crenellations above. In the western most embrasure there is a watch bell, called 'New Bell', which was once used for ringing curfews and alarms, and bears the inscription *In God is my Hope, R.B. 1605.*

NEW BELL or 'WATCH BELL'
This bell was one of three or four at different stations in the town which answered one another in ringing the watches or sounding alarms

In the combination of semi-circular (12th century Norman) and pointed (Early English and Decorated Gothic, 13th century and 14th century respectively) central arches below, the history of the development of this building is juxtaposed. These arches are again built in once grime-encrusted masonry, and serve as a poignant reminder of the era when the town

BARGATE
(South Side)
The whole of this front is the result of enlargement or refacing in the 14th century. The figure in the centre is of George III in Roman costume!

broker sat in the room above taking tolls and recording them in his brokage books. The kings and queens of England who passed through this space included Henry II when he came on foot in 1174 on his walk of penance to Canterbury, Henry V in 1415 *en route* to the Battle of Agincourt, and Queen Elizabeth I in 1591 when she visited Southampton with her entire court to be greeted by the Mayor and Corporation and presented with a purse containing forty pounds.

Perhaps the most fascinating event linked with the Bargate in medieval times concerns the alleged treason against Henry V, prior to embarking for Agincourt in 1415, by the Earl of Cambridge, Lord Scrope (or Scroop) and Sir Thomas Grey. A conspiracy concerning the duplicity of these men is narrated in Shakespeare's play *Henry V*, where in Act II, Scene II a council chamber depicts the room where the drama unfolds in the opening lines:

BEDFORD. Fore God, his grace is bold to trust these traitors.

EXETER. They shall be apprehended by and by.

WESTMORELAND. How smooth and even they do bear themselves as if allegiance in their bosom sat. Crowned with faith and constant loyalty.

BEDFORD. The King hath note of all they intend.

All three were tried and found guilty of taking bribes from the French and plotting to kill the King; as King Henry said to Lord Scrope 'that knewest the bottom of my soul that almost mightst have coin'd me into gold'. From the Court Room they were taken one by one to outside the Bargate and, in front of Henry's assembled army, were beheaded. The heads of Lord Scrope and Sir Thomas Grey were sent to York and Newcastle Upon Tyne and put on public display – no doubt to warn others of the rewards of treason against the king. Afterwards all three bodies were buried in or near St Julian's Chapel the worship place of the Huguenots in Winkle Street at the bottom end of the High Street. Inside this chapel there is a wall plaque which reads: 'Richard Earl of Cambridge Lord Scrope of Masham. Sr Thos Grey of Northumberland conspired to murder the King Henry Vth in the town as he was preparing to sail with his army against Charles the Sixth King of France for which conspiracy they were executed and buried near this space in the year MCCCCXV'.

Mention has been previously made of the **Guildhall** at first floor level, approached by a long flight of stone steps, where town guilds have met and where it was once customary for bands of strolling players to perform. Mayor makings also once took place in this room; the most dramatic of which took place in 1460 when a mob burst open the door 'with daggers drawn and menacing cries' thrusting their own candidate into the chair. Justices of the Peace also held court here until 1934. The prisoners consigned to the cells below were in turn responsible for some interesting carvings in about 1400, on the west jamb of the central arch.

The annual **Court Leet,** commonly called Law-day, was regularly held at the Bargate from 1617 until 1856. According to Dr Speed, Court Leet records, began in 1550 being an annual court to resolve disputes, originally held in the open 'at the cutted thorn' on Southampton Common. All the inhabitants of the town were required to attend on the third Tuesday after Easter 'on penalty of one penny for every defaulter'. Today Court Leet Presentments are still made to the City Council.

Without doubt the Bargate presents a powerful image and sense of place, marking unambiguously the site where the old town commences. These greatly sculptured stone walls on the north face, almost devoid of openings apart from narrow vertical slits of windows and a single entrance portal below, present an almost awesome appearance even today. One can understand the thoughts of the 17th century visitor who entered the town through this gate 'with no little fear'. In design and townscape terms, a positive statement of this kind greatly enhances the character of the city centre, notwithstanding its severance from the town walls by contemporary developments.

TOWN WALL

After discussing the construction of stage one of the Bargate in the 12th century, the development of Southampton's fortifications makes an interesting study, in particular in relation to the seaward defences to the south and west. By all accounts, these were initially neglected to allow ease of access to the sea for trade, and to maintain some important residences on the sea front. Great credence was given to the notion that the navy would adequately protect the town from a seaborne attack, and so the decision to embark on the construction of expensive protective walls was delayed. However, in 1338 there was a disastrous raid carried out by the French which left the town in ruins, after which King Edward III (1327-77) granted the town burgesses the right to 'take and collect upon all wares brought into the liberties of the said town ... one penny in the pound'. These funds were used to construct the great sea defences, much of which remain today. Subsequently however, the financing of these fortifications put a heavy burden on the town and therefore, in the reign of King Henry IV (1399-1413), 'the Mayor and Bailiffs and good men of our town of Southampton by way of aid for the fortifications ... two hundred pounds to be received yearly during our pleasure' to be provided 'out of the Duty upon Wooll, in the Port of the said town, by unit of the Privy Seal.' Thus it was that the fortifications were kept in good repair and provided with artillery, ammunition and gunners. In the reign of King Henry VIII (1509-47) it is recorded that limestone and chalk was brought from the Isle of Wight for ongoing repairs to these walls. The ravages of wind and rain from the prevailing south-westerly winds took its toll on the limestone walls and binding mortar, requiring this regular maintenance and repair, much as we see carried out today.

CASTLE EAST GATE
This gate gave access to Southampton Castle from within the medieval fortified town.

SOUTHAMPTON CASTLE

Castles as we know them did not exist before the Norman Conquest. Hitherto fortifications consisted of a wooden palisade on the summit of an earth mound, surrounded by earthworks in the form of a *Ha-ha* type ditch. After the accession of King William I, stone-built fortifications appeared, held under licence from the King. Their purpose to dominate and hold in subjugation the newly conquered people, while providing a safe haven for the feudal lord. Such a castle was built at Southampton on the north-west corner of what was to become the medieval walled town, directly adjacent to the sea. The site of the castle itself ultimately was to cover some three acres of land, and comprised the following elements at its zenith of development:

(1) a circular keep (on a raised earth mound) surrounded by:

(2) a curtain or bailey wall and ditch (to protect the inner bailey);

(3) two protected entrance gates, namely one on the sea side called *Castle Watergate* (not to be confused with the Water Gate at Town Quay) with another on the town side called *Castle East Gate*. The remains of both gates can be seen today, the *Watergate* set between the *Castle Vault* (to the north of the gate) and *Castle Hall* (to the south), while the *Castle East Gate* (now in ruins) lies in line with the present day Castle Lane.

(4) *Castle Quay* (separate from West Quay and Water Gate Quay, now referred to as Town Quay, to the south west and south of the Town Walls respectively). This quay specifically served the castle, landing and receiving goods for import (wine) and export (wool), both for the benefit of the monarch's household and the exchequer respectively. This quay would have also been used in part for the interchange of militia and armoury for the castle.

(5) At the extreme south-west corner of the castle there was a building called the *Garderobe* (built in 1252), which was in fact, for its day, a sophisticated self-

cleaning toilet arrangement, for the benefit of the residents of the castle. It would empty at low tide by a system of sluices, and was subsequently flushed out clean by sea water at high tide.

The date of the origin of the castle is estimated as some time between the Norman Conquest in 1066 and 1100, when the area covered by the layout was smaller than the final arrangement, as described previously. The position of the *keep* remained constant throughout, as did the Watergate entrance. It was the extent of the curtain walls and the shape of the protected baileys which changed. The main building period came in the late 14th century, when in 1378 (some time after the French raid of 1338) the architect and mason Henry Yevele was called upon to advise on the reconstruction of a new keep called *New Keep Tower*, during the governorship of Sir John Arundel. The main building and other works were completed by 1382. One William de Wyneford directed the work of the masons; tools and materials were assembled for the job, while the stone used came from such sources as Portland, Beer (Dorset), Purbeck and the Isle of Wight. (Stone quite often arrived as ballast for ships returning to

CASTLE WATERGATE
This gate provided the seaward access to Southampton Castle from the Castle Quay.

pick up export commodities.) Interestingly, records exist of the equipment used, including a *windlass* for hoisting heavy materials, and a *stone saw*. A lime kiln was also constructed on site to provide lime mortar for the stonework; this consisted of lime, sand and stonegrit aggregate. Apparently the contract for the keep was a rushed job, although work on the remainder of the castle continued at a slower pace, and was only completed in the year 1388. Unfortunately most of this structure is now lost to posterity, and we can only rely on glimpses of the past gleaned from the writings of those who saw the edifices at first hand.

Leland, writing in 1546, said 'the glorie of the castelle is in the dungeon keep that is both large and fair, and very stronge, both by worke and the site of it'. In 1599 Hortensio Spinola, in his report on southern ports, described the castle of Southampton as 'being strong with sixty pieces of artillery and 100 soldiers'.

Until about this time therefore, the castle was both the seat of government and defence in the Middle Ages but thereafter came its decline. How this came about is not quite clear, other than that redundancy had set in, for in 1650 one George Gollop granted the town commandant permission 'to take such stones from the Castle as he might think needful for the repair of the fortifications' (i.e. the Town Walls). Subsequently the site of the castle was parcelled to build town houses and their gardens, while in the early 19th century 'an extensive mansion of brick and stone' was built on the site by the Marquis of Lansdowne, which contained some remains of the old fortress. It was about this time that the novelist Jane Austen rented a shared house in Castle Square 'from the summer of 1806 until the spring of 1809' (the year the Marquis of Lansdowne died). Austen wrote of her house that it contained a 'pleasant garden, bounded on one side by the city walls; the top of this wall was sufficiently wide to afford a pleasant walk, with an extensive view, easily accessible to ladies by steps'. The mansion, built by the Marquis was apparently taken down in 1818 because it was said to be 'a fantastic edifice, too large for the space on which it stood, though too small to accord well with its castellated style'. Be that as it may, it was razed to the ground for scrap and the earth mound lowered, and in the year 1823 Zion Chapel was erected on the site of the Norman keep.

THE BLACK DEATH: EFFECTS AND AFTERMATH

The forty-year delay in the upgrading of the castle fortifications following the French raid of 1338 has already been commented upon. There were two reasons for this, namely the poor economic condition of the town of Southampton following the destruction of the raid, and the loss of confidence thereafter. But more significant perhaps was the emergence of the Black Death in 1348-1349, which is estimated to have killed about one third of the population of England in a two year period. Such an event obviously caused a shortage of labour, and those who survived found they could command a higher wage, whether working on the land (farming) or in the town (building), while King Edward III found significant difficulties in recruiting armies for his French campaigns.

The plague itself is thought to have entered this country via the small Dorset harbour of Melcombe (present-day Weymouth), carried by flea-infested rats, and thereafter the disease spread rapidly along the south coast to Southampton and elsewhere inland. Other theories abound on its source of origin but quite clearly the pestilence arrived here from the continent by sea, and medieval medical science was so primitive that man could but turn to God for deliverance, or so it seemed. Therefore the passage of trade through the Port of Southampton was reflected in the economic state of the town, and the Black Death demonstrated just how vulnerable the population could be to forces over which it had no control, or no knowledge.

There are some curious repercussions of this disaster in the buildings of the era. Some churches for instance will exhibit a complete change of style from Decorated Gothic (14th century) to Perpendicular (15th century) in the same section of the building, for no other reason than that work stopped, and started again some years later. Building skills similarly suffered with loss of expertise and use of inappropriate materials. Perhaps the most dramatic example of this is seen in the grotesquely twisted, timber framed spire of the Church of St Mary and All Saints at Chesterfield.

THE WEST GATE (AND ROYAL STANDARD INN)

Moving southwards along the Western Esplanade and past the Arcades, we come to the West Gate, which in the past provided the principal access to the West Quay. This mid 14th century stone tower is rectangular on plan and built on three levels. It comprises a central pointed arch and gateway at ground level, previously protected by two sets of double gates and portcullis, all beneath a stone barrel vaulted roof. There are two floors above, the first of which is reached by a long, single flight, stone staircase, and the second by an

THE WEST GATE
Through this gate armies passed to the battles of Crécy and Agincourt in the 14th and 15th centuries, while in the 17th century the Pilgrim Fathers left by this archway from what is now Westgate Street.

TUDOR MERCHANTS HALL AND THE WEST GATE.
This view, taken from inside the medieval walls, again reminds us of not only Southampton's long history but also nearer to the present-day, when the Tudor Merchants Hall was used as a temporary mortuary during the D-Day landings and after in 1944. Photograph by Peter Kilby.

internal staircase. The western face, looking towards the site of the quay, has rectangular gun embrasures on the first and second floors and a crenellated parapet above. The gate tower was built primarily for defensive purposes and does not seem to have been intended for residential use. The defences are solely directed towards the sea with no provision to protect the gate from attack from the side of the town. This gatehouse has two immediate neighbours on the Town Wall: the Royal Standard Inn, to the north and embedded in the walls, and the Tudor Merchants Hall, set behind the Town Walls and to the south. These two are separated by a flight of stone steps leading to both the first floor of the West Gate and the upper wall ramparts.

The **Royal Standard Inn** is a 19th century public house with a jaunty castellated facade, while the **Tudor Merchants Hall** (re-sited from St Michael's Square) was originally the Fishmarket on the ground floor, with the Woollen Cloth Hall on the first floor. The original building dates from 1428 when latterly it became a derelict structure, and in 1634 was sold to one Edward Exton for twenty marks (£13.33) when it was taken down and erected on its present site.

There are tremendous historical associations with the medieval port of Southampton including the embarkation of troops to fight in the battles of Crécy, Poitiers and Agincourt. When King Edward III was embroiled in the Hundred Years War with France, he was seemingly always outnumbered by the enemy when on French soil, with lines of communication stretched to the limit. However, the use of the longbow with its range of up to 250 yards (228.6 metres) and rapid fire capability had revolutionised warfare and led to significant victories. At Crécy for instance, the French had assembled an army of an estimated 40,000, while the English army was about one third in strength. On 26 August 1346, the French led by King Philip and the English by King Edward III who directed the battle from a high vantage point – while in the field his son Edward, just 16 years old and known as the 'Black Prince', was in the thick of the fighting. The attack by the French began at 6 p.m. but by nightfall some 10,000 had perished, brought down by the withering fire from the longbowmen. Similarly at Agincourt on 25 October 1415, although outnumbered by the French, King Henry V had scored a victory using the seemingly invincible longbow against the infantry and then the cavalry, the latter having made the fatal mistake of mounting a charge on a waterlogged battlefield which had turned into a quagmire, and ultimately a graveyard.

The departure of the Pilgrim Fathers is commemorated nearby, to the south of the West Gate, by the **Mayflower Memorial**. As recently as 3 October 1992, a plaque was placed here which reads 'In memory of Pilgrim Edward Doty, Mayflower passenger, 16th September 1620'. This simple but poignant inscription is a reminder of the heroism of these people, 101 in all, who in the reign of King James I set sail in the *Mayflower*, a vessel just 90 feet (27.43 metres) long and 25 feet (7.62 metres) wide, on a voyage which ended on 21 November in the same year. This is also the story of people who were driven to these extreme measures by either hopeless poverty or religious persecution. (On 16 August 1620 the *Speedwell* and *Mayflower* had set sail together from Southampton. The *Speedwell*, however, ran into difficulties and both ships put into Plymouth. The *Mayflower* continued alone from there on 16 September 1620 with the passengers from both ships crowded into one vessel, although some of the original party were left behind.)

BUGLE STREET AND ST MICHAEL'S SQUARE

Moving on past the Mayflower Memorial we arrive at Bugle Street, probably the most picturesque of Southampton's medieval streets, so named because of its association with the 'bull horn' used to warn of impending danger from the sea and elsewhere. There is so much that is historic that one can only select the most significant edifices for description; in any case the academic ground has been covered in great detail by previous writers. On the south-east corner is located the so-called **Wool House** (now the Maritime Museum), a robust and solid-looking stone building with distinctive cylindrical buttresses beneath a tiled roof, and some remarkable roof timbers in Spanish chestnut inside. Built in the 14th century, it was used to store wool brought from the West Country for shipment to Flanders, for cloth manufacture and distribution throughout Europe. Following the trade recession of the 16th century during the reign of King Henry VIII (1509-1547), its original use changed: in the 18th century it was used to confine French and Spanish prisoners of war.

Bugle Street is also remembered as marking the spot where the so-called French Raid of 1338 started, when on 4 October (a Sunday morning) ships landed on the hard known as 'the Gravel', opposite the Wool House and adjacent to the Watergate Quay (now Town Quay). The raiders advanced up the road and, arriving at St Michael's Square, burst into the church and slaughtered people at Mass. Minot, a contemporary poet, wrote of this event 'full fast they slew and burned'. The church,

ST MICHAELS CHURCH
The oldest church in Southampton open for worship, with its landmark spire reconstructed in 1877. Photograph by Peter Kilby.

having been so defiled, was afterwards visited by the Bishop of Sarum (Salisbury) in June 1339 to perform 'the office of reconciliation'.

St Michael's Church, standing as it does today in St Michael's Square (probably the most important urban space in the present day city), is the oldest church in Southampton. Dedicated to St Michael, patron saint of Normandy, it contains amongst its many treasures a carved black marble font of the mid 12th century brought from Tournai in Belgium. The church origins date from around 1066-76, the time of the settlement of French immigrants into the town. The focal point of this church is the central Norman stone tower with its massive semi-circular arches at the nave crossing, which are unusually devoid of ornament of any kind. Above this tower rises the smooth stone ashlar octagonal spire, dating from 1732 in the reign of George II and altered to its present form, when reconstruction added nine feet (2.74 metres) to its height in 1877. This spire is not only a landmark today but also served as an aid to navigation in medieval times and beyond.

The evolution of the plan form of the church makes an interesting study since its present rectangular shape, devoid of either transepts or porches, three-dimensional in its simplicity of silhouette, adds to the drama of the soaring spire above the roof line. Inside, the nave arrangement has changed gradually over the centuries, with aisles having been added to the Norman nave, i.e. north and south.

The nave proper was greatly reconstructed in 1828-9 when Francis Goodwin removed the medieval arcade and heightened the aisles to introduce galleries and additional seating. The overall result of this transformation is recorded outside, where we see quite clearly within the masonry profiles at the west end the outline of the previous triple gables with new stonework added above. Unusually, during the reconstruction of the nave, new pillars in cast iron, of a Gothic Perpendicular design, were added. However, in 1872 the relatively new galleries were removed because, by all accounts, their addition had resulted in serious structural difficulties and repercussions.

The date of the various elements of the plan starts in the 12th century with the Norman origin of the nave and tower. The chancel space also originates from the 12th century, the north and south chapels relate to the 13th century, while the windows in the north aisle wall are 14th century and the south aisle wall 15th century, as is the west wall in the main (some Norman buttresses mark the addition of the north and south aisles). This sequence *vis-a-vis* the north and south aisles again reinforces the theory of the adverse affects of the French Raid in 1338 and subsequent Black Death, both having caused a hiatus in building activities, epitomised by changes in style from one section of the building to the next, which might logically have been built at the same time. The progression of building dates and changes to this church is typical of the development of ecclesiastical forms, and therefore questions the idea that this element or that is 'original'; after the first stone is laid, every section is an addition and forms part of the overall evolution in which change is a constant factor.

Apart from the record of architectural change, St Michael's Church has ministered to the people of Southampton for 900 years or so. Contained within its walls are some poignant reminders of its history and people in the memorials, plaques and tombs. The church guide records that in 1160 King Henry II (1154-

1189) granted the monks of St Denys the patronage of St Michael, Holy Rood, St Lawrence and All Saints. This so held until the dissolution of the monasteries in 1537 and then passed to the Crown in the reign of Henry VIII (1509-1547). (There is a fifth parish, i.e. St Johns, and together each one is commemorated in the east window of the sanctuary).

Outside the walls in the confines of St Michael's Square is recorded as the location of the **Fishmarket** and **Merchants Woollen Cloth Hall** (now removed to the West Gate), marked by a diagonal line of toned paviours in front of the west door of the church. How noisy with the hustle and bustle of business this place once was! Old wine vaults pervade the area around St Michael's Church and Square, dating back to the prosperity of the wine trade era, and the settlement of an Italian colony of merchants who, in addition to the French, would have occupied some of the fine town houses in Bugle Street, until trade patterns altered in the 16th century.

Across the Square and facing St Michael's Church, we see the late medieval **Tudor House** (now a museum) fronting on to Bugle Street and at its junction with Blue Anchor Lane. Much has been written about this building but it is essentially a late 15th century timber-framed structure, built in an L-shaped configuration, backing on to a Tudor Courtyard Garden and the ruins of a Norman house named King John's Palace, set into and against the old town walls of the Western Esplanade sea defences.

Tudor House was built on the site of a previous house, to incorporate a banqueting hall, by Sir John Dawtrey of Petworth, who was Member of Parliament in 1495 and Sheriff of Hampshire in 1516. The house itself is built on three floors; the 'show facade' faces Bugle Street and exhibits the 'jetty' form of construction, i.e. it overhangs at first and second floors with quadruple gables at the top storey facing Bugle Street. These gables return at right angles at one end, giving the roof line a strong sculptural form. There are two entrances from the main road frontage:

the principal one to the right-hand side, is accentuated by a further overhanging jettied first floor single bay, and the one to the extreme left is the secondary and possibly the business entrance. Sir John was also the Kings Customer, in other words the Chief Customs Officer of the Port of Southampton. Originally there was a row of shops incorporated into the main frontage, but these were converted into parlours, while on the return frontage to Blue Anchor Lane, a buttery, pantry and kitchen were housed. Three main staircases exist giving access to the upper floors and bedchambers, while a further staircase connects with the vaults below. This house overall was very grand for its day, and exhibited the wealth and power of the first owner. When Sir John died in 1518, his widow married Sir Richard Lyster who was three times mayor of Southampton, and subsequently Lord Chief Justice of England from 1546 to 52, When he died he was buried in St Michael's Church opposite where his tomb stands today. In the courtyard behind the house lies what is called the Tudor Garden, once containing among its artefacts a bronze cannon presented to the town in 1542 by King Henry VIII.

Reference has been made to the so-called **King John's Palace** in Blue Anchor Lane, behind the Tudor House. Of this building Colin Platt has written 'in spite of its ruined condition, this house is still the most complete of the larger twelfth century town houses surviving in this country'. Basically we see here a two-storey house, with the ground floor given over to warehousing, and the first floor being the living accommodation, where there exists the remains of a Norman fireplace. Any connection with King John is both tenuous and conjectural, although it is quite possible that he may have stayed here in preference to Southampton Castle. The west walls of the house have been incorporated in the Town Wall, with the original openings blocked up to concur with the construction of the 14th century defensive system; new openings were made to form gun ports for small cannons, probably the earliest of their kind in Britain.

FRENCH STREET

Still in the French quarter we visit French Street and find another fine town house in the guise of No. 58, named the **Bulls Head Inn**. This house was built by one John Fortin, a wealthy merchant, in 1290, and is a timber-framed house on two floors with a collar purlin roof structure which extends beyond the end gable over the shop front to support the hanging sign. Below the two-storey shop, incorporating shop and parlour on the ground floor and a staircase leading to a gallery and bedchambers on the first floor, is a stone cellar or vaulted undercroft. Again this is one of the earliest surviving merchant's houses in England and, unlike King John's Palace, has been fully restored.

Retracing ones steps again back down French Street and to the Town Walls again, the next primary edifice can be seen in the remains of the **South Water Gate** facing the present day Town Quay. This gatehouse, now almost totally demolished,

BULLS HEAD INN 58 French Street. One of the earliest surviving merchant's houses in England.

would have protected the main access to the walled town from the south, and is on the axis of the High Street or English Street, as it was called. This gate is depicted on an engraving by S. Hooper dated 1784, which shows a two-storey gatehouse with a wide pointed archway entrance and embrasures above, surmounted by a tiled roof. To the left of the gatehouse one sees what appears to be a three-storey tower arrangement with windows which may have been part of the entrance arrangements, i.e. administration, for it was near to this gate and quay that shipbuilding activity was carried out. It was here in 1439 that one William Soper, a clerk of the King's ships, in return for repairing the South Water Gate at his expense, was given a 120 year lease at an annual tribute of one red rose! Prior to this period he had undertaken the task of refitting and building ships for the expeditions of Henry V (1413-22) against France. It was William Soper who at that time occupied the building in Porters Lane dating from 1170-1200, now named **Canutes Palace**, which used to serve as a ship's chandlery and house. In 1414 the Spanish ship *Seynt Cler De Ispan* was fitted out and renamed the *Holy Ghost* (714 tons). In 1418 the *Grace Dieu* (1400 tons) was launched here. A total of six ships to include also the *Gabriel* (1400 tons) and support vessels like the *Ane* (120 tons), *Valentine* (100 tons) and *Falconer* (80 tons) were built here, until the death of Henry V in 1422 brought this activity to an end. The Hundred Years War was a prolific period of shipbuilding, although Southampton had been on but the fringes. The main centres were London on the Thames and Portsmouth; shipwrights were imported from these centres by Soper to carry out the work in Southampton, which was the base for the merchant navy as opposed to the royal navy. (It was not until the 18th century that men-of-war were built in some profusion in Hampshire by Henry Adams, on the Beaulieu River at Bucklers Hard.)

HIGH STREET (ENGLISH STREET)

In the High Street (formerly English Street), entered through the Watergate, two significant medieval buildings are situated, namely the Red Lion Public House and the remains of the Holy Rood Church. The **Red Lion Public House**, although much restored, is as Colin Platt states 'an important example of the late medieval Hall House and Shop'. This 15th century timber-framed building has a deep rectangular plan and at three storeys high on the main frontage, all above a stone undercroft, it makes maximum use of the site. Originally there was a shop on the ground floor at the front which led on to the hall element. This in turn reached the full height of the building, with a 'unique gallery' on the north side above the ground floor, through an access passage. This room, known as the 'Court Room', is where circumstantial evidence suggests that the three conspirators were tried for treason against Henry V, although perhaps this location is a case of mistaken identity - who can tell?

HOLY ROOD CHURCH
Dating from 1320 - now a stabilised ruin, memorial garden and chapel for the Merchant Navy.
Photograph by Peter Kilby.

Holy Rood Church stands further north on the same side of the High Street as the Red Lion. Blitzed in World War II, the church now stands as a stabilised ruin and memorial garden and chapel for the Merchant Navy. Holy Rood was one of the three English churches in medieval Southampton. Originally the building was situated in the middle of the High Street, but in 1320 was rebuilt on its present site. It was from this church that the town assembly bell was heard heralding early morning and curfew at night. Today the tower still stands, as do the surrounding walls, with the roof open to the sky. The timber spire which once adorned the tower fell during the town's air raids in the 1940s. It is recorded that once a west porch was placed facing the High Street, called the *Proclamation House,* for announcing important town events.

ST JULIAN'S CHAPEL, GODS HOUSE TOWER AND THE TOWN DITCH

Of the other remaining medieval churches in the town, at the bottom of the High Street in Winkle Street is St Julian's Chapel, the Huguenot church of Southampton. the chapel leads on to the 14th century **Gods House Gate**, immediately adjacent to the 15th century **Gods House Tower**, constituting the south-east corner element in the medieval town defences, of which David Lloyd writes 'built in the early 15th century to protect the sluice which controlled the flow of water into the extra-mural defensive ditch' i.e. to the east of the Town Wall, on the landward. Again this gatehouse is three storeys in height with a doubly protected arched gate, i.e. portcullis, and gates as described for the Westgate fortifications. Gods House Tower served also as the headquarters of the town gunner in the 15th century, having been built for artillery also, hence the display of inverted gunslots on the east and north elevations. This fortification marked the commencement of the **Town Ditch** which protected the east and north walls of the medieval town. This man-made water feature completed the protection afforded by the sea on the south and west extremities of the fortifications. Of this element Colin Platt writes 'certainly by the mid century [13th] a bank and a ditch, the former crowned with a timber palisade, or even a light wall, enclosed the town on its northern and eastern flanks'. Looking at the layout of Southampton in the late Middle Ages, the Town Ditch was certainly a major feature of the town's defences, crossed in only two places by the entrances

ST. JULIANS CHAPEL
- in Winkle Street
View of the chapel from Gods House Tower.

to East Gate (now lost) and the Bargate itself to the north. A minor access called Friars Gate was built in 1373-74 to give the friars entrance to their gardens outside the town walls and to play bowls.

Gods House Gate and Tower were so called because of the proximity of the Hospital of St Julian, founded in the reign of King Richard I (1189-1199) by Gervaise Le Riche, 'burgess of Hampton'. Royal protection was given to this foundation by King John (1199-1216) as did Henry III in 1234. King Edward III confirmed the previous gifts

The East Windows of the chapel.

in 1332 and in 1343 'granted custody of Gods House to the Provost and Scholars of Queens Hall Oxford' as well as the provision of almshouses for the care of 'afflicted scholars'. Subsequently in 1462 King Edward IV gave a grant by charter to 'secure increase of divine worship within the Hospital of St Julian or Gods House'. Today therefore we see the evidence of this religious foundation in the shape of St Julian's Chapel, dating from 1195, outside which is written 'St Julian Eglise Francais. Services Le Dimanche 11 heures du matin et 3 heures l'apres midi. Octobre 1 1866. Rev. A.A. Dupont Pasteur Mars 25 1878.' Alongside this chapel today are two blocks of almshouses, one for men and the other for women.

THE VAULTS

In addition to all these artefacts we see above ground, i.e. the fortifications, buildings and churches of the medieval town, lie hidden a complex of stone vaults and

QUILTERS VAULT - in the High Street. A 12th century stone built vault associated with Southampton's wine trade.

subterranean structures which might be classified as 'architecture below ground'. Some of these structures have already been commented upon in relation to the castle, Tudor House, 58 French Street and the Red Lion Inn for example. However, in addition to these we see the majestic **Quilters Vault** on the west side of the High Street, dating from the 12th century it is typical of the vaults in Southampton connected with the wine trade, carried out from the time of the Norman Conquest until the demise of England's lands in France in the 15th century, during the reign of Henry VI. Another such example is the **Undercroft** at the junction of Simnel Street and Bugle Street. The chamber itself is made up of two bays of ribbed stone vaulting, probably built in the year 1320. Unlike the wine vaults of the town, this vault is supposed to have had another purpose, namely providing accommodation for pilgrims *en route* to the shrines of Winchester and Canterbury.

The full life of the medieval walled town and its fortifications is thought to have lasted until the reign of Queen Elizabeth I who died in 1603. The change in fortunes of the town at this time has been put down to the loss of the Italian trade, but the town nevertheless kept its Customs House and port facilities in good order, and prepared itself for new social and economic forces to take hold. The decline of the town defences had a positive side, in that a feeling of peace and security reigned after the defeat of the Spanish Armada. The subsequent granting away of the castle by King Charles I marked the end of one era and the beginning of a new period of development when the security of the town walls was no longer of prime consideration, and so the expansion outside these confines began to gather pace.

Metz del. Walker sculp.

The POLYGON near SOUTHAMPTON.

Publiſhed as the Act directs, by Harriſon & C.º July 1,1783.

"POLYGON HOUSE"
This engraving is an artists impression of the ill-fated polygon development of the Spa period in Southampton's history. The remains of which and foundation stone dated "9th August 1768" are still to be seen embedded in the Polygon Hotel. Reproduced by courtesy of Hampshire County Library Southampton Special Collections.

3. THE 'GOLDEN AGE' OF THE SPA AND RESORT PERIODS

In the early 18th century the combination of the medicinal qualities of natural springs found in the town, allied with the bracing effects of sea bathing, brought about the rejuvenation of an ailing economy and the establishment of Southampton as a fashionable spa resort. In 1746 mineral springs were discovered at the bottom of Bargate Street in Spa Road. Chalybeate water, containing compounds of iron and sulphur, was thought to contain healing properties boasted as being parallel with those of Royal Tunbridge Wells 'but of double power'. In a poem entitled 'Economy of Beauty' written in 1770, we hear 'love the sole disease the waters cannot cure'! Perhaps the definitive quotation on the subject however refers to the water's properties to help those 'afflicted with rheumatism, hyponchondrical afflictions and debilities ... , from too tender indulgent and inactive way of life'! Be that as it may, the town grew in reputation as a desirable place to live and visit, both to see its attractions and to be seen, as it were. It was at this time therefore that Southampton started to grow, not only in social reputation but also in size, beyond the limits of the medieval town walls.

The extent of Southampton in the early 18th century was hardly greater than in the century before, with comparatively few houses outside the town walls. All this was to change however, because whereas in 1774 it was estimated that the total number of houses in the town centre amounted to some 705, by the end of the century this number would have doubled in parallel with the growth of the spa activities, leading on to what has been called the 'Resort Period'. It was at this time also that the erection of large houses began in Above Bar Street, being the very first of the significant developments which were to take place outside the enclave of the medieval walls. From this situation there were easy walks or 'promenades' to the sea front of Western Shore, and for the more adventurous, northwards via Bellevue Place (now London Road) leading to the common and the countryside beyond.

LONG ROOMS

Alongside these developments several facilities were built to satisfy the needs of both the wealthy and the leisured classes. In 1761 baths were constructed by John Martin at West Quay which were filled and emptied by the tide, allowing about five hours' bathing each day. Alongside this facility a room was added for bathers and patrons to enjoy taking tea, playing cards, and attending balls three times a week. A great deal of decorum was associated with these events, to the extent that entrants to society were vetted first by the Master of the Ceremonies, and that as a part of his duties he would draw up and enforce rules of precedence. For instance we read in 'Regulations at the Southampton Summer Assemblies in 1781': (1.) Gentlemen were not to appear in the rooms on Tuesday, Thursday or Saturday evenings in boots; (2.) They were always to leave their swords at the door; while Rule 5 states that dancing in coloured gloves is not allowed! In conclusion it states 'Ladies and gentlemen coming into the town were asked to leave their names and places of abode entered in one of the Long Room books, or at Skelton's Circulating Library and to offer the Master of the Ceremonies some occasion of being presented to them'. In order to submit to all this discipline a subscription of £1.1.0 was required to be paid for membership, with additional expenses for attending the various functions. Such was the success of these events however, that further additions were made to the **West Quay Baths** in 1766 and 1767, when the whole building became known as the *Long Rooms*. These rooms faced the Town Walls, their entrance being almost opposite Blue Anchor Lane. The contemporary accounts paint a picture of rarefied luxury within this establishment, 'fitted up with pier glasses' and musicians' bandstand.

THEATRE IN FRENCH STREET
This engraving depicts Mr Collins 'THEATRE ROYAL' which was built at the end of the 18th century and after an illustrious history was destroyed by fire to be replaced by the NEW THEATRE ROYAL in September 1880. Reproduced by courtesy of Hampshire County Library Southampton Special Collections.

Other forms of indoor entertainment included masquerades, usually held in the Great House in the Polygon or in the Long Rooms, as well as live theatre. In 1766 a small theatre was built in French Street by subscription. Fifteen sponsors paid ten guineas each for this to be done, but by 1780 the building was already too small and was therefore enlarged. In 1798 however, the manager, a Mr Collins, had even more ambitious plans and bought St John's Hospital in the same road, erecting a new theatre on the site called 'The Theatre Royal'. Provincial touring companies performed here who included Portsmouth, Chichester and Winchester in their circuits. An engraving of the theatre shows a simple two storey structure with a rendered facade and parapet of classical design, indicating a piano nobile at first floor level, which presumably held the auditorium. In the early days of the previous theatre building, it is recorded that in 1773 Goldsmith's play '*She Stoops to Conquer*' was performed before the Duke and Duchess of Gloucester, – an event which produced a packed and enthusiastic audience.

COACHING INNS

In addition to the attractions of the spa activities in relation to the development of Southampton, the emergence of stagecoach travel, combined with a regular postal service by the same mode of transport, improved communications from one part of the country to another, and in so doing helped to stir to life a hitherto stagnant economy. The coaching inns which remain to this day, like the Star and Dolphin in the High Street (English Street), bear witness to this phenomenon. A guide book published in 1781 sets out the timetable and itinerary of Collier's Stage Coach to London, which left the Star Inn at 5.00 a.m. each day (except Sunday) and travelled via Farnham with a stop for dinner, to arrive at Ludgate Hill in London at 7 p.m. for disembarkation at the Belle Savage Inn (the fare to London amounted to 10 shillings). Goods traffic was also carried by road in 'wagons', while mail was transported by stagecoach, the average speed of which was twelve miles per hour with a change of horses at regular intervals. Also along with this form of transport came the delivery of newspapers from London: the *Morning Chronicle* and the *Morning Herald*, which could be purchased at Fords Circulating Library in the High Street. This era saw the emergence of an elementary system of public transport before the coming of the railways, together with the means of dispersal of information by post and newspapers, using methods which would allow this source of knowledge to become more universally available.

'GENTLEMEN'S PARTY'

The social forces at work in this so-called 'spa era' became manifest in the influx of a new stratum of society dubbed the 'Gentlemen's Party', which sought to bring about changes in the way the town was being managed. There was, for instance, no tangible form of regulation as to where and how buildings were erected. The maintenance of highways was hitherto a personal affair, in which each owner was responsible for the area between building frontage and a point at the centre of the road. Pavements as we know them did not exist, there was no street lighting other than that afforded by individual houses. All this was to

AN ELEGANT LAMPPOST outside the courtyard entrance to the Dolphin Hotel.

change however, when an act of parliament in 1770 gave authority to council members to pave footpaths and town carriageways, erect street lamps, and build 'watch houses' for policing after darkness. This act was in effect the precursor of local government, also heralding the naming of streets, numbering of houses, and the issuing of bylaws which were transmitted by either the town crier or on handbills. Surprisingly, modern traffic regulations ensued, banning the obstruction of the

STAR HOTEL (formerly the Star Inn)
A Richard Singleton was 'tenant' of this hotel in 1601 although like the Dolphin Hotel, its origins go back to the 13th century.

highway by tethered horses, carriages and carts left standing, which could be impounded on default, and secured to a tree in Above Bar – hence the origin of present day Pound Tree Road. In parallel with these changes and the town's increasing popularity, the condition of properties generally began to improve and were enlarged to provide visitors accommodation, not least of which were the coaching inns. These can be highlighted here for their ability to accept both travellers and visitors who intended to stay on for the 'season'.

The two coaching inns which remain in the High Street, namely the **Star Hotel** (formerly the **Star Inn**) and the **Dolphin Hotel**, are recorded as existing, in part at least, at the beginning of the 17th century and so link the spa period of the 18th century with the medieval period of the old town, which can conveniently be assumed to have ended with the death of Queen Elizabeth I in 1603. In addition both buildings, while displaying a differing elevational facade to the High Street, have nevertheless a common characteristic in plan form of an arched entrance at the front, giving coaches access to the once cobbled courtyard area and stables at the rear. At the Star Hotel there is a stone plaque at the front which reads *Coach to London, Sundays excepted, Alresford Alton, performs – 10 hours* – an early example of a travel timetable in contrast to the ever changing computerised displays at the railway stations and airports of today. Both inns, now hotels, have a fascinating history. The Star Inn is referred to in an early document of 1600 in the Winchester College Deeds as the 'tenement belonging to the Priory of St. Denys', forming the northern boundary of property owned by the college.

In 1601 a Richard Singleton was the tenant, and it is also recorded that a Mr Kingston was alleged to have blocked off 'a very ancient light into the cellar of Richard Singleton of the Star'. There was originally a long garden behind the Star, and the 1771 map shows this feature with a small road called Star Inn Lane, running alongside and to the south leading on to the back of the walls to the east. Moving forward in time to 1831, it is also recorded that the then Duchess of Kent stayed there for several days, accompanied by the twelve year-old Princess Victoria; the Mayor and Corporation presented their compliments, and in return were thanked for 'a most cordial reception'. To this day the coat of arms of Queen Victoria remains high above at the front of the building. In its present form the Star Hotel presents a four-storey facade to the High Street; the lower three storeys date from before 1800 and the fourth storey was added and the whole stuccoed between 1830 and 1840. There is a projecting balcony across the whole front at first floor level, with six windows behind at this same level, as well as a large, three light central window and stuccoed fanlight under a segmental arch. All in all, the hotel is of a contrasting design to the Dolphin Hotel situated lower down the street on the same side and to the south.

The first mention of the Dolphin Hotel comes in documentation from the year 1267, and again in the great survey of 1454, where reference is made to 'Le Dolphyn' as belonging to the Wardens of the Parish Church of Holy Rood. Later in 1648 John Taylor, 'a roaming poet', wrote on passing through the town:

> 'with fiery speed the foaming bit they champed on
> and brought us to the Dolphin at Southampton',

while in 1796 Mary, Viscountess Palmerston, drove over from Broadlands at Romsey 'and danced at the Dolphin'. Later there were associations with Queen Victoria, who left her carriage and horses there while on her way to Osborne House, her beloved home on the Isle of Wight. The Dolphin Hotel is an extremely handsome and architecturally elegant building of *circa* 1760, with distinctive bow windows at first floor level each side of the central balcony to the first floor windows above the segmental arched opening to the yard behind. Within this 'yard' and to the right (the south) is a 16th century timber-framed two-storey stable block, with some recently restored framing and brick noggins, again to the south, all under an oak-

DOLPHIN HOTEL ('Le Dolphyn')
There has been a hotel on this same site since the 13th century, although the oldest part of the present building is the 16th century stable block at the rear. The existing main facade dates from around 1760.

framed and tiled roof. Inside the main hotel there are some very fine rooms, namely the entrance hall with an 18th century carved stone chimney-piece, and a staircase leading to the first floor dining room at the front, with coved plaster ceilings and a fine pair of carved stone fireplaces.

These two fine buildings, the Star and Dolphin Hotels, epitomise the formality of a polite and organised society in 18th Century Southampton, and bear witness to the elevated patronage they received in their heyday of that period. The nature of the architecture and contrasting styles of both buildings is a also reflection of the new order which had resulted from the intervention of the 'Gentlemen's Party', raising the standards, expectations and reputation of the town.

POLYGON DEVELOPMENT

The need to provide a suitable residential development for the new monied classes moving into Southampton is instanced by the ambitious development in the vicinity of the Polygon Hotel. To the south and west of the main facade of the contemporary structure we find an inscribed foundation stone stating: 'This stone (being the first of the Polygon) was placed 9th Aug 1768 By The Rt Hon'ble Viscount Palmerston and The Rt Hon'ble Hans Stanley of Poulton' This inscription confirms the location of the development proposed for twelve up-market houses on a site of some twenty-two acres (8.9 hectares) of land, laid out on a circular plan with an outer carriageway and tapering gardens converging to a central complex of a hotel and shops. Plans were drawn up by an architect called Jacob Leroux according to a client's brief which had been provided by the then developer Isaac Mallortie, with General John Carnac providing finance. Apparently, however, Southampton was not yet ready for a development of this scale and class, and unfortunately just three houses and the hotel were built; the overall enterprise fell into insolvency. Following this, three more of the houses of the

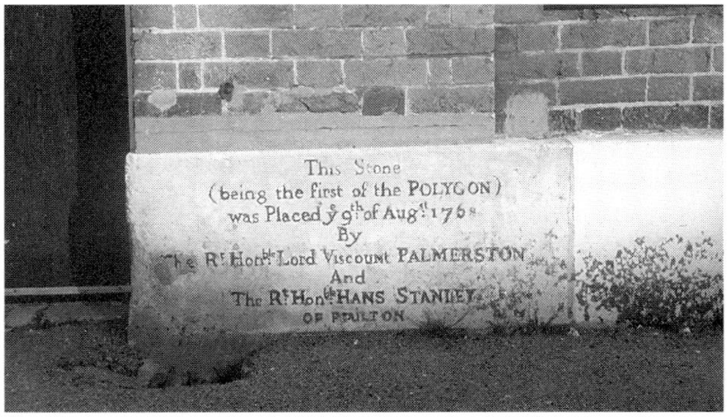

The Stone Plaque recording the foundation of the ill fated Polygon Development.
Photograph by Peter Kilby.

original scheme were built, making six in all, and today the only evidence we see of this project are some remains of the original elevations built into the side facade of the modern hotel, in the location of the foundation stone. Nevertheless, the Polygon district remained a select residential area from the eighteenth to the early nineteenth centuries, as the developments to the north of the old town moved out from Above Bar Street to join the suburbs.

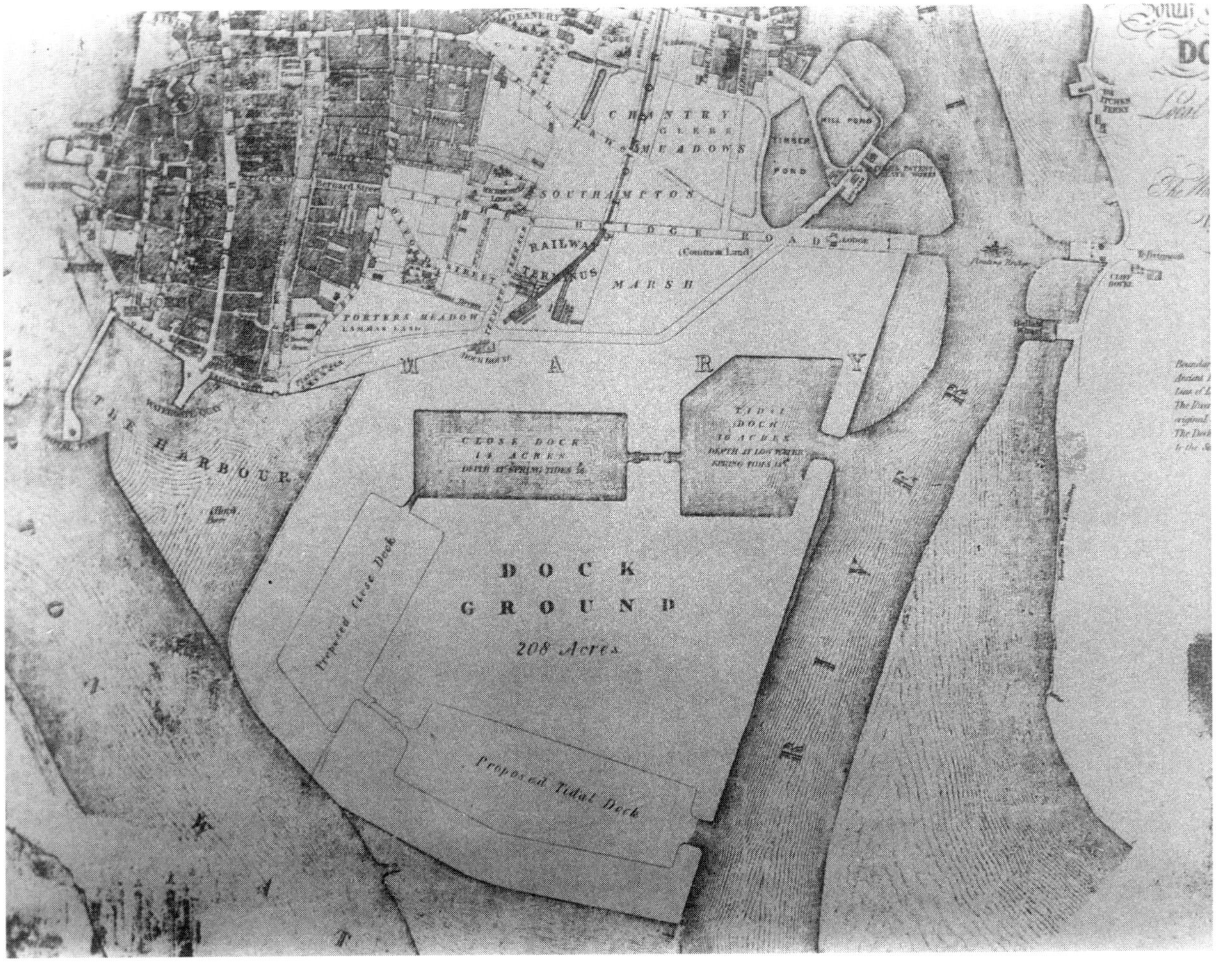

MAP OF 1870.
This shows the layout of the Outer (Tidal) and Inner (Close) Dock completed in 1842 and 1851 respectively.

4. SOUTHAMPTON DOCKS: THE OLD AND THE NEW

The history of the foundation of the Southampton 'Old Docks' in 1838 is inextricably inter-related with the coming of the railway, and together these two events had a significant and far-reaching effect on the economy and development of the town. For centuries the mercantile activities of the port had been carried out from West Quay and the Water Gate Quay, but in the beginning of the 19th century land reclamation began on the vast mud flats to the west of the Itchen Estuary leading into Southampton Water, to form what was to be called the Outer (Tidal) and Inner (Close) Docks, completed in 1842 and 1851 respectively. The location was in the vicinity of the sea frontage alongside Platform Road and Canute Road, on a site now occupied by the modern development of Ocean Village. The land was achieved by filling in the Inner Dock, and creating a marina from the Outer Dock, now known as the Princess Alexandra Dock, where today pleasure craft and ocean-going yachts sit at their moorings. The total development of the area of the Old Docks occupies a roughly triangular peninsula of reclaimed land, spreading its tapering finger out towards Southampton Water, bounded to the east by the River Itchen and to the west by the Red Funnel Terminal, Town Quay and the sad remains of the once splendid Royal Pier. These later elements form a small harbour, of which the point of contact with the dry land is the only place where the sea is near its original boundary position. This harbour presents a delightful view when looking down ancient Bugle Street at the sight of the ferry vessels and the sparkle of the blue waterfront. In addition, the harbour marks the boundary between the Old and New Docks; the latter, when viewed across the green expanse of Mayflower Park to the west, stretches right along the Test Estuary until the Redbridge Causeway is reached.

Before the creation of both the Old and the New Docks by placing materials dredged from what is now called the 'Dredged Channel' upon the existing expanse of mudflats, the sea had lapped against the walls of the medieval town. This gave access to the old Town Quays, while along the full length of the Millbrook Shore, the sea again ruled supreme, maintaining the aura and character of Southampton as spa and watering place. Maps of Southampton from 1846 illustrate the shoreline at that time, while engravings of the day by Philip Brannon in 1850 show quite clearly the uninterrupted expanse of the Millbrook Shore looking in the direction of Freemantle. Another engraving, looking towards the Test Estuary from 'the Quay and Victoria Pier' (Royal Pier), confirms the waterline as being hard against land which in the next century was due for reclamation and development to provide the site for the world-famous King George V Dry Dock, opened in 1933. It is to the east of the Royal Pier and in the vicinity of the South Western Railway terminus that we must turn our attention, in following the development of the Old Docks, and in particular the buildings which now line Canute Road immediately adjacent. During the 'halcyon days' of the Spa Period this area became known as 'The Beach', being on the line of a bank thrown up to protect an area of common land known as the 'Saltmarshes', to the east of the old town. In 1844, however, all rights of common were removed when the Marsh Improvement Act was passed, thus allowing development to occur along the curving line of Canute Road itself, in response to pressures for 'commercial exploitation'.

Without doubt the most imposing and interesting of the buildings in Canute Road is the **South Western Hotel** (now called South Western House), completed in 1872 and designed by the architect John Norton, having been built by the London and South Western Railway to accommodate liner passengers. Situated on a prominent corner site, it was originally L-shaped in plan, allowing the railway itself to terminate inside, as shown on a map of 1870 when it was called the Imperial

THE SOUTH WESTERN HOTEL (Now South Western House)
Designed by John Norton, in its original form it is perhaps the most spectacular of all Southampton's listed buildings of the Victorian era. Photograph by Peter Kilby.

Hotel. The design of the building both outside and inside can only be described as extravagant, reflecting the wealth and prestige of the port at that time, and latterly, with further additions in the 20th century, it represents the flowering of the liner trade at its zenith. The interior is particularly ornate and especially beautiful for its period, with marble used extensively in the public areas, elaborate ironwork on passenger lift shafts, and really fine, spacious corridors providing access to the rooms. Of special interest today is the old Summer Dining Room on the ground floor, which faces Canute Road, with its high, semicircular headed cast-iron framed windows and, at high level, a mural on canvas of the Pilgrim Fathers setting sail for

A MURAL DEPICTING THE MAYFLOWER AND PILGRIM FATHERS
Situated in the summer dining room of the South Western Hotel, this painting was recently discovered during refurbishment work and was restored by the artist A. Scott-Moncrief.

TITANIC
This photograph, taken from an old postcard, shows the liner before its first and last voyage, tied up at Southampton Docks.

the new world. The entire building is steeped in history of events and important visitors, and is sadly linked with the unfortunate passengers of the *Titanic* who stayed here before that fateful voyage. In the quietness of the stairs and corridors today, one senses a feeling of the ghosts of those who perished when the liner sank amid the icebergs of the North Atlantic.

The hotel building is linked to the original station terminus building by a fine glazed canopy of steel and glass, and together these three elements make an imposing group, the power of which is matched only by the **Goods and Engine Shed** in St Lawrence Road

GOODS AND ENGINE SHED
This fine building in St Lawrence Road was part of the original Southampton Terminus complex of the London and South Western Railway and has recently been restored as part of a student housing complex for the Southampton Institute.

immediately opposite, across the still existent rail link to the docks. This great engine shed, spanned by spectacular steel girders with vast triple brick arched openings at one end to allow goods trains to run in under cover, was originally designed by the architect Sir William Tite in the mid 19th century. The building can rightly be described as a cathedral to transportation and commerce, and its pure scale and power is quite breathtaking when viewed from within, now with its gleaming, newly-painted steelwork, restored multi-russeted brick walls and vast, new glazed roof. It is a poignant example of how a historic building in a recently ruinous state can be restored to a condition of equilibrium and well-being.

On the Canute Road frontage nearby there is a delightful run, again of newly-restored buildings, with Victorian shop fronts and a mix of rendering and brick elevations, leading on to the **Canute Castle Hotel**, to complete this frontage. Built in 1850 in response to the needs of the docks, it makes a bold statement with its rendered facade and classical pilasters, topped originally by an octagonal observation area at roof level, once giving a view directly on to the sea and the New Forest beyond. A plaque on this building records the reproving by King Canute of his courtiers for their flattery, and by failing to hold the tide of the sea at bay, demonstrating both his humanity and his humility.

Immediately on the other side of the road are a series of mainly brick buildings, backing on to the docks, each one with its individual history and character. The buildings on the southern side of Canute Road, to the west of Dock Gate No. 2 and along to Dock Gate No. 4, represent in the main official and international maritime concerns. These opened in response to the development of the docks, following the laying of the foundation stone at a great ceremony in 1838, the year after Queen Victoria came to the throne of the United Kingdom and the 'Empire'. Immediately adjacent to Dock Gate No. 2 (now the entrance to Ocean Village) is situated **Ferry House**, built *circa* 1870 in Beaulieu white bricks

CANUTE CASTLE HOTEL
A plaque on this buildings reads ...'Near this spot ad1028 Canute reproved his courtiers'
Photograph by Peter Kilby.

FERRY HOUSE
The original headquarters of the Southampton Dock Company.

CANUTE CHAMBERS
This building with fine Dutch Gables was the home of both the American Line and the White Star Line. It was to this place that the distraught families of the crew and passengers of the Titanic came to hear news of their relatives.

under a Welsh slate roof. It is a typical example of a Victorian office docks building, originally erected to house the headquarters of the Southampton Dock Company, and so it remained the nerve centre of the dock and its railway-related activities, until the Dock Board of the time moved to new premises in 1964. On the east elevation of this building the entrance door carries either side finely calligraphed memorials to the fallen in two World Wars.

Immediately adjacent to the west is the red-brick building of **Canute Chambers**, with its decorative tiled roof, built in 1893 to house the offices of the American Line. In 1907 the famous White Starline joined forces in the same building. It was to this place that the distraught families of the crew and passengers of the *Titanic* came to hear news of their relatives caught up in that historic maritime disaster. In 1931 the United States Line moved into the building, so continuing the tradition

DART HOUSE
Home to the North German Lloyd Line (NORDDEUTSCHER LLOYD) until 1914.

DART HOUSE
A detail of the pediment.

of the liner trade for which the name of Southampton has been synonymous.

Further along to the west in the same road we see **Dart House**, built in 1899 as Maritime Chambers to house the North German Lloyd Line (Norddeutscher Lloyd) until 1914. In 1919, after the hiatus of the war, Cunard opened their Southampton office to be joined in 1934 by White Star, forming Cunard White Star. It is not an altogether distinguished-looking building, being of heavy proportions in yellow brick (recently cleaned), with the logo of the London and South Western Railway within the pediment, recording the name of the owners of the docks at the time.

Perhaps the most interesting building along this stretch of road is the diminutive single storey **Wilts and Dorset Bank**, built in 1907 with a classical stone facade and the name cut into the entablature in finely carved trajan roman lettering.

Finally to the **Union Castle House** designed by Alfred Giles, the Docks Engineer, and built in 1847 as the Custom House. It is probably the most

WILTS AND DORSET BANK
This classical stone facade faces Canute Road.

UNION CASTLE HOUSE
Designed by ALFRED GILES, the Docks Engineer, and built in 1847 as the Custom House.

architecturally correct building in the street, with its low profile of two stepped storeys of stone on the ground floor and yellow brick above with brick rusticated quoins, under hipped tiled roofs with great wooden modillion cornices. The overall composition is stabilised by the central louvered lantern and lead-domed cupola. Inside there are some beautiful spaces and classical features reminiscent of the elegance of a bygone era. In 1890 this building was taken over by the Union Steam Ship Company, who merged with the Castle Line to form the Union Castle Line in about 1899, and stayed thereafter in this building until 1982.

These several buildings on the south side of central Canute Road are exampled as representative of the maritime architecture of the period, catering for the administration of the docks and shipping lines, as well as banking and the official activities of customs. Mostly these buildings are utilitarian rather than beautiful, although as has been suggested, both the Wilts and Dorset Bank building and Custom House have an aura of elegance over and above the needs of function and utility.

Returning now to the development of the docks operation, the ancient quays, i.e. West Quay and Water Gate Quay (later Town Quay), were essentially dry at low water. To some extent the construction of **Victoria Pier (Royal Pier)** in 1832-3 overcame this problem, especially when it was extended in about 1890 to designs prepared by 'Mr Farley of Edinburgh' which provided berths for about 'eleven steamers', together with provision for a pavilion, restaurant and club house for the Royal Southampton Yacht Club, as well as a bandstand and seating for several hundred people at the Pier Head. As for the design, a newspaper article in the *Hampshire Independent* states 'every detail here, as indeed throughout the whole pier, is highly ornamental, and in illustration it may be mentioned that the brick piers of the offices will be surmounted by lions bearing the Southampton Arms'. Sadly today, however, little remains of this edifice apart from the pier substructure

VICTORIA PIER (ROYAL PIER)
Opened by Princess Victoria on 8 July 1833.

of 'screw piles with rolled iron girders and iron bracing, the floor being wood', because the beautiful superstructure buildings of the Pavilion and Mayflower Rooms have been swept away by fire. The cast-iron superstructure itself was constructed in elegant cast-iron columns and roof members, the columns being fluted and surmounted by Corinthian capitals constructed in four sections and bolted together, providing an early example of pre-fabricated construction and modular co-ordination techniques. As for the formation of this pier, it was set up to accommodate the steam packets plying between Southampton and the Isle of Wight (as used by Queen Victoria *en route* to Osborne House), the Channel Islands and the Continent, while giving direct access to the railway system with a consortium-type arrangement between the South Western Railway and the Isle of Wight Steam Packet Company. Fortunately the **Pavilion** at the pier entrance, built in the early 20th century, still remains and this elegant domed structure, although at the time of writing in need of repair and maintenance, is another reminder of the elegance of the pier's structure which once lay beyond and behind. Also remaining are the 'brick piers ... surmounted by lions' as referred to earlier. By the very nature of their position, these piers may be at risk from plans to forge a route through to the proposed Eastern Docks in the road immediately adjacent. As a postscript and epitaph to the Royal Pier, its activities for pleasure once included concerts, drama and dances, and even roller skating. Oh happy days!

As previously stated the Royal Pier served to accommodate smaller passenger steamers plying to the Isle of Wight, the Channel Islands, and the Continent, but it was unsuitable for larger vessels and had no provision for repair services. In recognition of the need to provide deep water berths for larger vessels and the need to link these facilities to the newly formed railway system to London, it was suggested in 1831 that the London and Branch Railway Company should also form a dock company, but at that time it was forbidden by law that railway companies could own steamer companies. However, in 1836 an act of parliament allowed the then Southampton Dock Company to construct new docks on 216 acres (87.41 hectares) of mud flats adjacent and to the east of Town Quay. Surveys for their

TRAFALGAR DRY DOCK
Opened in 1905 on 21st October to celebrate the centenary of the BATTLE OF TRAFALGAR.

KING GEORGE V GRAVING DOCK
Opened in 1933 and still operational, it was to this dock that great liners like the QUEEN MARY and QUEEN ELIZABETH came for their annual refit.

construction were carried out by Alfred Giles, and later on his death, his son took on the task of Docks Engineer in 1846. At this time trade routes to the Far East were expanding and Southampton became recognised as a more convenient stopping-off point than London, assuming that the right facilities were in place. Thereafter followed an intense period of land reclamation and construction of the so-called '**Old Docks**', commencing with the Tidal Dock (now called the Alexandra Dock and serving as marina to Ocean Village). Sixteen acres (6.47 hectares) in area, it was opened in 1842 to receive both the SS *Tagus* and the SS *Liverpool*, owned by the Peninsular and Oriental Steam Navigation Company. The need to transport mail and troops to and from the outreaches of Queen Victoria's Empire created further need to expand the docks' facilities, and in 1890 the aptly named '**Empress Dock**', was opened personally by the Queen. This new dock provided a quay frontage of 3800 feet (1158 metres), and more importantly the facility, to allow vessels of deepest known draughts to enter and leave at any tide.

As for the provision of repair facilities, dry docks were built culminating in the construction of the **Trafalgar Dry Dock**, which was opened on 21 October 1905 to mark the centenary of that famous sea victory of Lord Nelson and his fleet. This dock is vast today, and in 1913 was the largest in the world. It now looks like a great inverted cathedral in the ground, green, rust-covered and derelict. What use is there now for this unwanted dinosaur of a bygone era, splendid though it may be?

Finally in 1911 **Ocean Dock** (originally named White Star Dock) was opened, giving a further 3800 feet (1158 metres) of quay space, in an alternative configuration to the Empress Dock.

Throughout the period of expansion, more and more shipping lines changed their allegiance to Southampton, but with the advent of the Great War in 1914, the port was placed under government control and served thereafter as a military embarkation port. During the following years until 1918, it sent literally millions of men with their equipment and materials to fight in the bloody and costly conflict in Europe.

As a postscript to the Old Docks, mention can be made of the old **Post Office Building** in Platform Road, adjacent to Dock Gate No. 4 and opposite the beautifully tree-lined Queens Park. This three-storey brick building with stone quoins and a hipped slate roof was built in 1902 as a custom house to replace the older Custom House of 1847 (now Union Castle House nearby). In its increased size it bears witness to the vast increase of trade and movement through the docks between the time that the foundation stone was laid in 1838 and the end of the 19th century.

WINDWARD TERMINAL
A fine PORTAL ARCH and entrance to the New Docks exhibits a plaque which reads '1939-1945 This tablet was presented to the Southern Railway by the 14th Major Port United States Army, in proud and glorious memory of the men and women of the forces of the United Nations who sailed from this port during the great war against aggression, to ensure the freedom of mankind.'

This expansion of trade is reflected in the increase in the town's prosperity and in an era of almost unrivalled growth of its buildings, both residential and commercial, linked with the railway of which we will talk later (in Chapter 5).

Further to the west, past Town Quay and the Royal Pier, lies the vast 'New Docks', again built on reclaimed land, alongside the Millbrook Shore until its boundary with the Redbridge Causeway. At the entrance alongside Mayflower Park at Dock Gate No. 8, beneath the portal arch of elegant fairfaced concrete with monumental brick piers each side, the **Windward Terminal** commences, marked at its waterside by a low-slung brick building (housing a pump house to the town's stormwater system). Through this entrance gateway passed troops bound for the D-Day Invasion of the Normandy beaches in 1944, an event marked by a plaque on the gate piers. These docks serve two primary purposes, as a container terminal and a berth for present-day ocean-going

A CONTAINER SHIP
One of the regular sights on Southampton Water. Photograph by Peter Kilby.

liners. Primary vehicle entrances are seen at Dock Gate No. 10 with the monumental **Rank Hovis Flour Mill** and Dock Gate No. 20 forming a link with the Millbrook and Redbridge Roads, and M271 connection beyond.

It is in these docks both old and new that the heart-beat of modern marine commerce now pulses. The statistics for the Port of Southampton over the past ten years or so highlight the peak figures for each item over the decade. For instance, in 1991 25 million tonnes of oil were handled. In the years 1988 and 1991, 172,000 vehicles were imported and 223,000 exported. The score for 1988 is 600,000 containers, a phenomenal figure. Passenger traffic peaked in 1993, with 214,000 passengers on cruise liners, and in the following year nearly two million passengers were carried to the Isle of Wight. In 1994 the total traffic of cargo goods (excluding oil) amounted to nearly eight million tonnes!

Shipping movements in and out of the port in 1994 totalled 54,488, of which 8,423 were piloted. Some of the largest figures in these statistics include 5,483 tankers, 1,598 container ships, 34,046 Isle of Wight ferries, and interestingly in peacetime, 1,047 military vessels. These figures all bear witness to the life and vitality of the port today, living up to a history which goes back some 2000 years to the first site at Clausentum in Roman times.

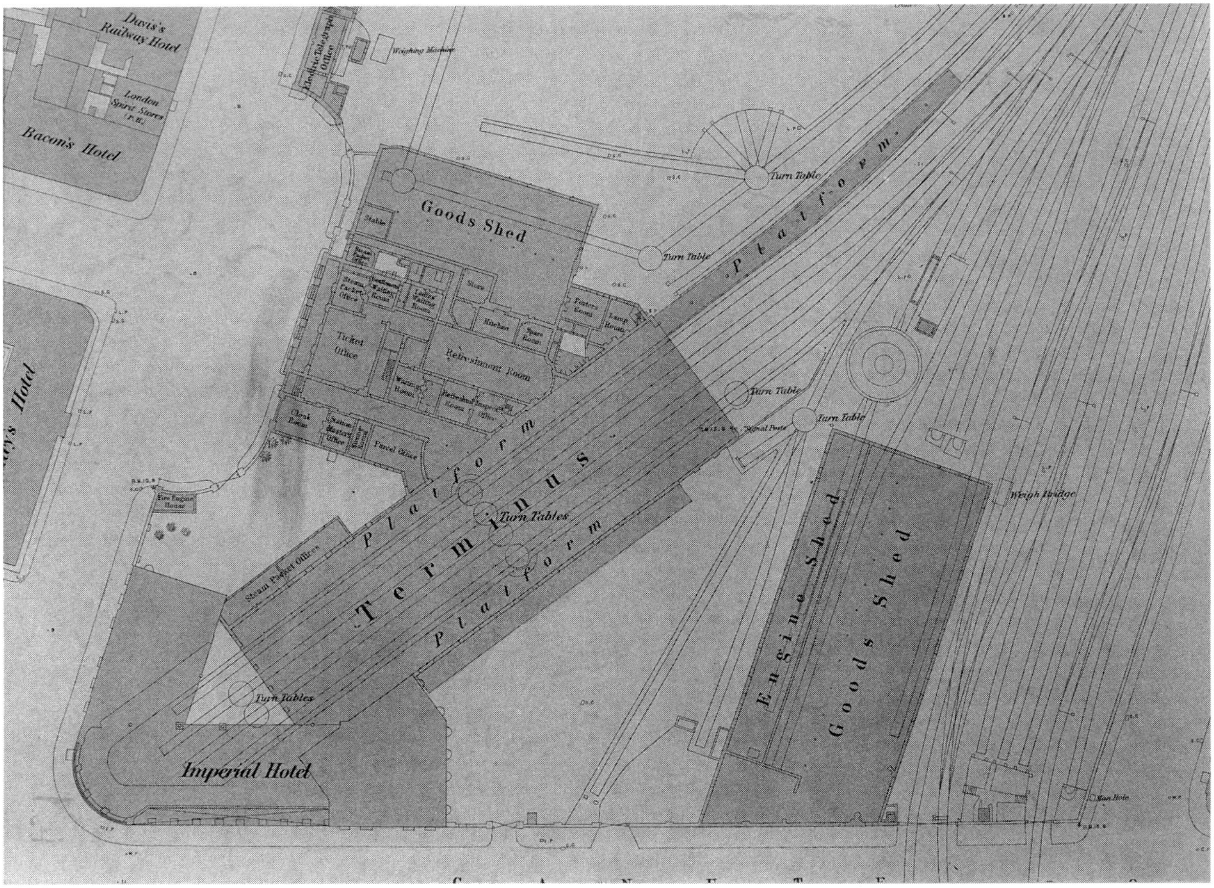

MAP OF 1870. This shows the railway terminating inside the Imperial Hotel itself (later the South Western Hotel). Note the plan of the Terminus Station and goods and engine shed, the latter to be rebuilt on its present site. Reproduced by courtesy of the Ordnance Survey.

5. THE LONDON AND SOUTH WESTERN RAILWAY AND THE ILL-FATED CANAL

When the London and South Western Railway (formerly the London and Southampton Railway) opened in May 1840, linking the capital with Southampton (and its docks), it heralded a new era in the mode of transportation and set in motion a series of social and economic developments which were to change the face of not only Southampton but the country at large.

Work had started on the railway link in 1836 and was carried out in a series of sections. The London to Woking Common link was opened on 12 May 1838, a distance of 23 miles and travel time of 45 minutes. A year later, the Southampton to Winchester section was finished in May 1839, as was the line from Woking to Basingstoke. Engineers and their gangs of labourers were forging the final link, and the whole track was complete from London Nine Elms to Southampton Terminus. Initially there were no stations between Southampton and Winchester; St Denys and Swaythling stations were to be built later, before the end of the century. In a railway timetable for the **London & Great Western Railway** published in October 1848, there are ten trains a day leaving Southampton for Waterloo, the earliest departing at 1.25 a.m., and arriving at 4.30 a.m., and the last departing at 6 p.m. and arriving at 9 p.m. The fastest trains were the two expresses, one leaving at 9.15 a.m. and arriving at 11.15 a.m., and the 1 p.m. getting there at 2.50 p.m a journey time of just one hour and 50 minutes! Fares for the express trains were 21 shillings for a first class single fare, and 23 shillings and sixpence return; second class cost 15 shillings single fare and 18 shillings and ninepence return. Bearing in mind the train travel times against those for the stagecoach as recorded at the Star Inn, i.e. 'coach to London, Alresford and Alton performs in 10 hours', it was inevitable that the first casualty of the coming of the railway would be the stagecoach, as well as the inns and service stations along its routes. Another notable casualty, although before and not directly associated with the railway, was the ill-fated **Southampton to Salisbury Canal** project. Planned and built in part between 1794 and 1808 during the reign of George III, this was a brave idea to link the wharves on the waterfront at Northam on the River Itchen with a canal. This canal was to run parallel with the River Test to Redbridge, and then eastward to Michelmarsh and finally north to Salisbury. Before the advent of the railway, all goods were transported by road or shipped by water along the coasts and rivers. A purpose-built canal, clear of any obstructions save for the locks and bridges, and also free of the vagaries of wind and storms at sea, was considered to be the best option by the enthusiasts wishing to emulate the success of the Manchester Ship Canal of 1761. However, there was much criticism of the idea of a canal built alongside a river, i.e. the Test, although the counter argument to this was to say that a purpose-built canal avoided the navigation problems of negotiating mud flats between high and low tide water levels.

In 1794 however, an engineer named Joseph Hill was commissioned to design a canal system to link Southampton with Salisbury, in the manner previously described. His plans were costed in 1794 and in the following year tenders were sought from contractors. From day one there were problems with the project, not least of which arose from the failure of the District Committees, which were set up to manage the project, to agree on plans for the progress of the work. The original estimates, on which the capital expenditure had been based, were found to be too low in practice, and eventually the project was abandoned unfinished.

A map of Southampton dated 1851 shows the line and progress of the railway lines through Southampton and its suburbs of the time. How then was this railway born? In November 1833, Francis Giles, a civil engineer from London, produced a plan of the intended London and Southampton Railway, which was incorporated in an act of parliament in 1834, giving authority to such an undertaking. This

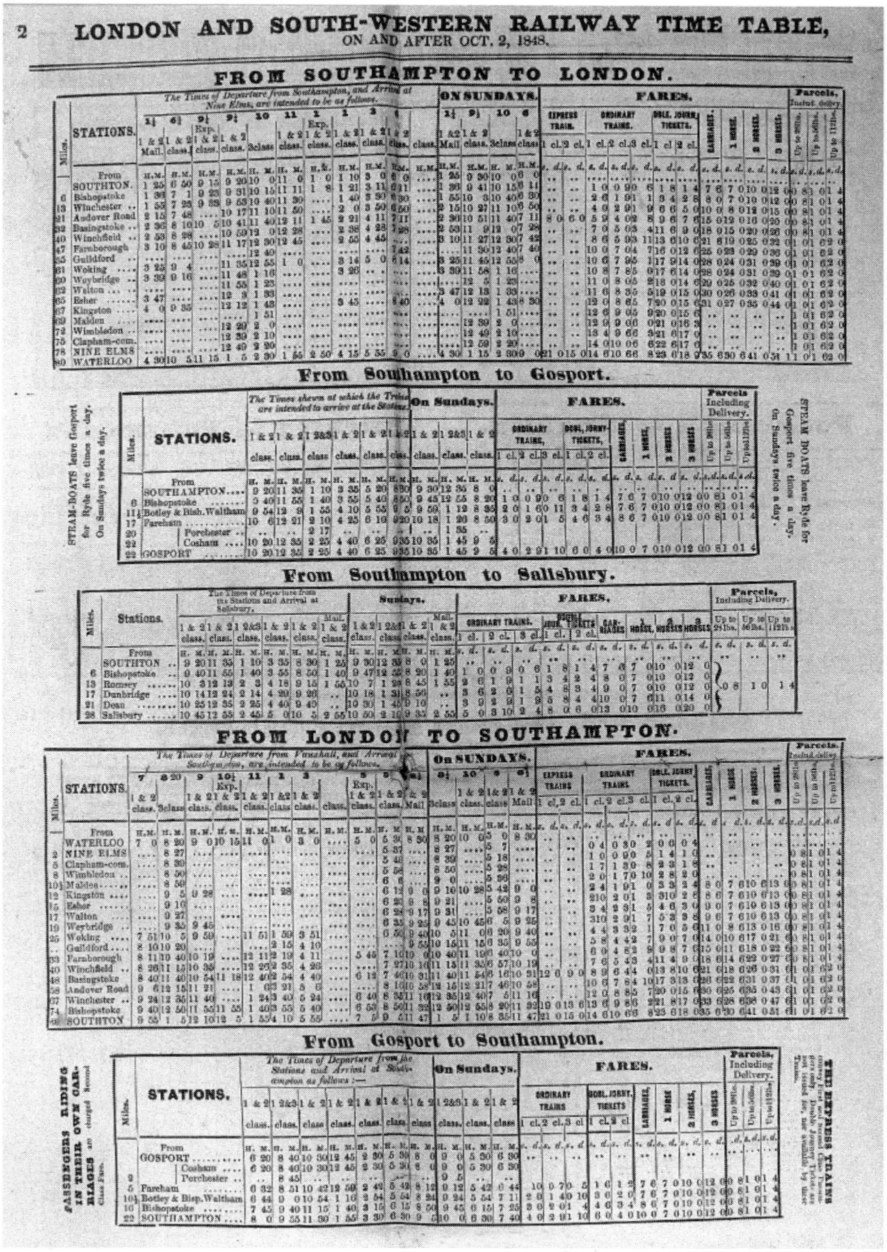

2 LONDON AND SOUTH-WESTERN RAILWAY TIME TABLE,
ON AND AFTER OCT. 2, 1848.

FROM SOUTHAMPTON TO LONDON.

From Southampton to Gosport.

STEAM-BOATS leave Gosport for Ryde five times a day. On Sundays twice a day.

STEAM BOATS leave Ryde for Gosport five times a day. On Sundays twice a day.

From Southampton to Salisbury.

FROM LONDON TO SOUTHAMPTON.

From Gosport to Southampton.

PASSENGERS RIDING IN THEIR OWN CARRIAGES are charged Second Class Fare.

RAILWAY TIMETABLE An epitaph to a bygone era.
Reproduced by courtesy of Southampton Archives Services.

railway was to commence 'at the River Thames at or near Nine Elms, in the Parish of Battersea in the County of Surrey, to the Shore or Beach at or near a place called the Marsh, in the Parish of St Mary in the town and county of Southampton', for the purpose of the transit of passengers and goods. The planned route of this railway was through a corridor of land 'not to exceed 22 yards', affecting literally hundreds of properties and ownerships. Land for the purpose of building the railway was to be acquired by a system of compulsory purchase, in which owners were compensated for their loss, and for which there was an appeal procedure for those who were aggrieved.

The act itself laid down procedures for the management of the railway, and set down design criteria and specification requirements for the engineering. For instance, it states of the railway bridge over the River Itchen, 'each arch shall be of sufficient dimensions to admit the passage thereunder in the deepest part of the channel of a barge, the lading of which measures seven feet and one inch in height above the surface of the water ...', and continues 'to admit the passage upon the towing path under such arch of the horses used for towing-barges in the said navigation'. Provision is also made for obstruction of the waterway during construction on penalty of £6 for every 24 hours of the offence. Of the railway carriages, it stipulates that they 'shall be constructed agreeably'. Similarly it is stated that 'the locomotive and other engines ... should be under the control of the said company'. In other words, all engines and rolling stock were to be regularly inspected in the interest of public safety, and the owners made responsible, whose names were to appear on the coaches in white or gilt lettering two inches high! Speed limits were set, and it was forbidden to drive cattle or horses along the track. For enforcement special constables were appointed, being the forerunners of the Railway Police.

Because of the new and divisive nature of the railway track, owners of land on either side were empowered to build bridges, fences and drains, etc., at their own expense. In order to further protect the interests of the public at large, it was stipulated that 'engines were to consume their own smoke'!

In order to finance this vast enterprise, the Southampton, London and Branch Railway and the Dock Company issued a prospectus, with a view to raising £1,500,000 share capital by the issue of shares at £20 each. Having designed the railway in a thoroughly professional way, details in the Company Prospectus suggest that the feasibility study of the enterprise was carried out in a similarly efficient way. The general thrust of the economic argument was that it was cheaper to import and export goods via Southampton Docks and to transport them by rail, than by continuing the sea voyage to London. 'Was it for the purpose of bringing the ships to London at such vast expense, most certainly not ... the ships were not wanted in London but the cargoes were!' extolled Colonel Henderson in his speech to the shareholders in the Town Hall at Southampton in 1831. Annual exports and imports of various commodities had been analysed to include coffee, corn, cotton, cocoa, wines and spirits, etc., with national exports alone valued at in excess of £36 million per annum in 1828; these statistics were used to indicate that a proportion of this total could well pass through the proposed 'safe and commodious docks and warehouses' in Southampton. Calculation of the profits to be gained from the transport of passengers and goods by railway were then estimated at £120,000 per annum net, being a ten per cent return on the initial outlay, i.e. less than the share value of the company flotation of £1.5 M.

THE BUILDINGS

At the commencement, the **Terminus Station** at the Southampton end of the line was opened in 1840, to the design of Sir William Tite. The station itself is closed today and is now a casino. However, the building remains intact, built on two levels

TERMINUS STATION. Opened in 1840 to the designs of Sir William Tite

with the highest at three storeys and the lower alongside: a two-storey wing with rooms in a mansard roof. The building is distinctly classical in style with arcading on the ground floor and entrance doors set back behind the arches, affording protection from the elements. There is a rusticated stucco wall on the ground floor with, in effect, imitation stonework; the walls behind in the recess are in buff bricks, probably Beaulieu 'whites'. The ornate entrance doors are more like glazed screens. At first floor level in the main block we see pedimented windows, and above on the second floor there are some simple sash-windows, with a delicate dentil feature underneath the sills, while above all this is a classical cornice and entablature. This distinctive building, together with the remaining steel-framed and glazed canopies which served the original platform, forms a link with the South Western Hotel built later. It was certainly most worthy in stature and design to serve as the terminating building to this historic railway linking London with the Old Docks, and the rest of the world beyond.

ST DENYS STATION

ORNATE BRIDGE AT ST DENYS STATION

Two further stations were built on the Southampton to Winchester stretch of the line, at St Denys in 1866-8 and Swaythling later in 1883. Both would have been built in response to the expansion of the town into the suburbs, which began in earnest after the railway (and the docks) came to Southampton in 1840. **St Denys Station**, the earlier of the two, is a somewhat elaborate affair, not only because of the main station building on the 'upside' of the line, but some equally fine brick buildings on the central platform, reached by ornate iron footbridges complete with fluted cast-iron supporting columns and classical capitals. The main station building is on two storeys in a balanced classical design, with four-pane sash-windows with moulded head, jambs and sills on both the ground and first floors. These are set into a rich red brick wall with rusticated quoins beneath a simple cornice feature and pitched slate roof. The single storey buildings, as mentioned for the central platform, again are in red brick, with a horizontal string course line in buff bricks – probably from Beaulieu – while the window and door openings are resplendent with precise, rubbed brick arches with very fine joints and stone key and springing members. There are also some beautiful terracotta medallions set high up in the brickwork, while the station canopy has the usual vertical scalloped, painted boarding and patent glazed roofs, supported by flamboyant and brightly-coloured cantilevered cast-iron brackets. Outside the station is the South Western Arms public house on the down side, and the Dolphin outside the main entrance (now interrupted by a new road). There is now a somewhat sad, 'end of an era' feeling about both this station and Swaythling, further along towards London. Both stations now appear to have outlived a full and useful life, although they are still operational and extremely elegant nevertheless.

Swaythling Station has a more domestic appeal in its appearance, with its brick walls and Dutch gable, sash-windows and tiled roof not higher than one storey, uncomplicated and unsophisticated in design. Again we see arched brick lintels, and this time brick keystones (as opposed to stone); the window openings are trying to look bigger than they really are, with their seemingly massive and out-of-scale moulded sills. The booking hall has a high ceiling of boarding and purlins to a pitched timber roof, and moving through a substantial brick arch and ornamental iron gate, we arrive on the platform. The canopy to this is supported by utilitarian iron stanchions with some fairly ornate (although less so than at St Denys) cantilevered brackets. Outside there are two adjacent inns, one closed, and the other near the railway arch over the main road, the Fleming Arms, open. Just as the stagecoach was a casualty of the railway, these intermediate stops between the main line stations have less importance now with the advent of the motor car, and to some extent public road transport, dealing with short and most commuter journeys.

Returning to the 1851 map, we see that the railway not only branches outwards to both the main docks and those at Northam, serving the wharves at Millbank, but just south of New Road it now curves westwards towards the tunnel beneath the parks, towards the original **Blechynden Station**, now replaced on a different site by Southampton Central (originally called West Station). This line opened in 1847 and went westwards as far as Dorchester, hence its name the 'Dorchester Line'. This railway, passing as it did along the Western Shore, is immortalised in the engraving by Philip Brannon which shows the sea lapping the beach immediately alongside the track; this same railway now leads westwards to Weymouth. The spirit and energy as well as the innovation of this Victorian era of the railway seemed to expand the population in leaps and bounds, on to new horizons. It was certainly a period of monumental growth, but still held on to the past. This is epitomised by the 1848 railway timetable which under 'fares' makes provision for taking one's horse on the train; one horse to Winchester is quoted as costing seven shillings, two at 10 shillings, and three for 12 shillings – it makes one think!

HOUNDWELL
HOGLANDS

6. THE VICTORIAN ERA

With the death of King William IV in 1837 and the accession of Princess Victoria to the throne, so began an almost unparalleled era in British history, with the expansion of the Empire throughout the world. It is significant therefore that in 1841 shortly after Queen Victoria's accession, the Ordnance Survey was to transfer its Tower of London headquarters to London Road in Southampton. A survey of the whole of England for military purposes had commenced in 1791, following the work of Major General William Roy in the 1780s. Pioneer of the land triangulation survey technique, Roy had inaugurated a historic scientific experiment on Hounslow Heath (within the vicinity of present-day Heathrow Airport) to ascertain the difference in longitude between the observatories of Greenwich and Paris. (An iron canon at the Kings Arbour site at the airport marks the north west terminal point of the first baseline of Roy's survey in 1784.) Of this event it is said 'the fact that such a matter could generate an international debate at all, illustrates how the Scientific Community of eighteenth century Europe maintained close contact over national frontiers.' In order to prove a point, it was proposed to set up triangulation grids on the ground from Greenwich Observatory to the coast at Dover, and to link up with French triangulation points across the Channel in the vicinity of Calais. The exercise had strong associations with the science of astronomy, and formed the basis of large-scale accurate and systematic map-making as we know it today. This form of survey was also to be linked with the introduction of known levels above the so-called Newlyn datum, where all land levels are inter-related

EXTRACT FROM 1846 MAPS
Surveyed in 1845-6 by Sergeant W. Campbell and 'a detachment of the Royal Sappers and Miners under the command of Capt. W. Yolland R.E.' These maps record in detail the state of medieval Southampton before the changes brought about later in the 19th century. Reproduced by courtesy of Ordnance Survey and Southampton Archives Services.

PLAQUE AT ORDNANCE SURVEY BUILDING
One of several plaques recording the progress of the building works on this site.

throughout the country to a mean sea level. The marking of these levels on maps and on the ground was achieved by the provision of a series of bench-marks, seen usually on immovable objects like stone walls and marked by an arrow pointing upwards to a horizontal line.

The responsibility for the map-making process was assumed by the Board of Ordnance, the origin of which can be traced back to the Middle Ages and the establishment of the Royal Arsenal in the Tower of London. 'The primary responsibility of the Board of Ordnance ... was to act as custodian of the lands, depots, and forts required for the defence of the realm and its overseas possessions.' It is from the hands of military surveyors that we inherit the fortifications and harbours which were to protect this country's 'invasion coasts' in Tudor times and beyond. It is fitting, therefore, that such an organisation should set up its new headquarters in the vicinity of what was once a fortified medieval sea town.

The original buildings on the London Road Ordnance Survey site were built as barracks in about 1800, and were therefore laid out in military order around parade grounds and still functioned as a military-type establishment while trained soldiers carried out much of the hands-on field work during the course of the

WESTERN RANGE OF OFFICES
The world famous Ordnance sheets were produced here until 1969.

survey exercises. A new building was added to the complex in about 1841, namely the **Director General's House** on the corner of London Road and Rockstone Place. The whole group of buildings became depleted as a result of air raids in about 1940, but those parts which remain are resplendent in classical details and proportions, carried out in the characteristic 'local' Beaulieu white bricks with natural slate roofs and fine sash-windows.

It was from these buildings that maps were to be produced until the Ordnance Survey moved to the present modern offices in 1969. The survey of England in 1791 already referred to was to produce maps to a scale of one inch to the mile, while in 1841 the detail was increased to six inches to the mile, and in 1854-5 the scale was again increased to 25 inches to the mile. Perhaps the most interesting and detailed maps we see from that era are the 'Sixty Inches to One State Mile' maps of Southampton in 1846, surveyed in 1845-6 by Sergeant W. Campbell and 'a detachment of Royal Sappers and Miners under the command of Capt. W. Yolland, RE'. These maps, beautifully produced in colour, give a highly detailed plan of the buildings and gardens, and with shadow lines create an almost three-dimensional, realistic effect. In addition, and most significantly, the maps also show the internal plan layout of the key buildings, and a particularly fascinating view of the medieval walled town, with its castle, ancient quays, and churches with their parish boundaries. In addition, the materials of these buildings are shown, i.e. stone or brick houses in pink, and wooden houses in grey. Over and above all this detail, wood pavements are shown in black, and macadamised or gravelled roads in light brown, as well as services, water and gas pipes and sewer lines. Finally, levels above datum are indicated by the formal bench-mark notation. These maps, then, represent an encapsulation of history; they are the first systematic and *scientific* representation of the layout of the town of Southampton before the changes to its topography were brought about by the coming of the railway and the opening of the docks.

Map-making before the 19th century had been primarily a private affair, as exampled by the map of Southampton of 1842, published by Geo Doswell, land surveyor and civil engineer, to a scale of 132 yards to the

A STYLIZED VIEW OF VICTORIAN SOUTHAMPTON
Published in the Illustrated London News in 1844 drawing signed "Smyth". Note the proximity of the sea to the walls of the old town. Reproduced by courtesy of Hampshire County Library Southampton Special Collections.

inch. One of the earliest maps of Southampton on record is an Elizabethan map of about 1560 (but now thought to be later). This map in full colour is a more stylised view from the air showing buildings and landscape, ships and water, together with the general topography of the sites of Clausentum, St Mary's Church and the medieval walled town and quays, with the area of Southampton Common to the north. This map, however, is not to scale, and the same comment applies to Speed's map of Southampton of 1611 which is at best a keyed diagram of the old town and its relationship with the site of Hamwic and St Mary's Church. Mazell's map of 28 August 1771, 'published according to Act of Parliament', is a much more accurate affair showing the street pattern of the walled town, the extent of the salt marshes, St Mary's Church and the location of the departure point of the Itchen Ferry, together with a key inset plan of the proposed ill-fated Polygon development.

Maps of Southampton also exist dating from 1791, 1800, 1802 and 1835, as well as the Geo Doswell map of 1842 to which we have already referred. These maps give a sequential view of the development of the town up to that date, but it was during the reign of Queen Victoria that the town grew dramatically with the coming of the railway and the founding and expansion of the docks. A new and expanding economy financed a seemingly vast building programme of commercial, residential and ecclesiastic buildings, the arrangement of which was recorded in such detail by the new map-making techniques. More importantly, substantial government and military resources were made available for this work to proceed at the Ordnance Survey offices.

BUILDING SUPPLIES

As a rider to this corollary, it should be remembered that, in order to progress large scale development of any kind, both land and resources need to be available, the land having been assembled by the developers and surveyed, and designs produced. The availability of building materials close at hand at affordable prices is a further prerequisite. In October 1842, T.C. Elliott, 'Merchant and Commission Agent', set up business on Millbank Wharf on the west bank of the River Itchen, for the sale of 'Roman Cement, Plaster of Paris, Stone ... and Ground Lime'. In addition to these materials, slate was imported and an agency set up for supplying stucco and paints for rendering. Thus it was that Elliotts was founded, and so remains until this day, although it is now a group of companies dealing in building commodities.

In addition to this facility, there already existed a brick works close at hand at Beaulieu, home of the famous 'Beaulieu Whites'. These bricks were manufactured from since 1790 at Baileys Hard Brickyard on the Beaulieu River in Hampshire, where production continued until 1935. Other notable sources of brick supply existed later on in the name of Blanchards at the Bishop Waltham Kilns, founded in 1862 to produce, in addition to bricks and roofing tiles, high quality and 'artistic' terracotta ware in various colours, but mainly red and blue. Production on this site continued well into this century until the yard closed in about 1956.

Another important source of supply were the brickyards at Bursledon, established in 1897 and closed down thereafter in 1974, producing beautiful red bricks in their heyday. The brickworks today have been saved from demolition by the Hampshire Building Preservation Trust and are being restored as a museum and study centre for building materials.

Without doubt the Beaulieu kilns, producing both 'whites' (actually a light buff colour) and 'reds', were in operation at a critical time in the development of Southampton, and were able to serve the needs of the 19th century building programme. The brick making process at Baileys Hard was based on the local availability for the brick-making process for making both 'reds' and 'whites', coupled with the ready supply of timber from the forest for firing the kilns (before the availability of coal in 1870) and the proximity of the Beaulieu River to provide water transportation of the finished bricks to towns like Weymouth, Portsmouth and Southampton, each with its sea frontage. Three barges were used for this work, namely the *John and Samuel*, the *Kitty* and the *Louisa*, each capable of carrying a delivery of 16,000 bricks or thereabouts. On the return journey they carried chalk quarried in the Isle of Wight, for use by local farmers.

The brick-making process itself was highly labour-intensive and involved firstly the digging of clay by hand, to be left out of doors for 3-4 months for 'weathering'. Then followed the 'pugging' process, i.e. mixing of clay with water (and lime for the whites only) to achieve a texture suitable for brick-making and moulding. This was first done by hand and then in 1854 by machine to keep pace with production demands and escalating orders from builders. The moulded bricks, now sized 4 $^{1}/_{2}$" x 9" x 2 $^{3}/_{4}$" (11.4 cm x 22.9 cm x 7 cm) with a top 'frog' (indentation),

125 HIGH STREET (HOLY ROOD CHAMBERS)
A fine building in seemingly Germanic gothic style. Built in 1888 in brick and terracotta, it is crowned by stunning ornate chimneys.

would be stored for about a month then fired for about four days and allowed to cool for a further two days, before removal from the kiln. This controlled process produced bricks of high reputation and performance, not only in their strength and durability, but also in their retention of their fine colour.

These bricks were used in many important buildings in Southampton and throughout the country. The Beaulieu Archives at Palace House record that Mr Hooper of Southampton, a builder, was ordering loads of 20,000 bricks a day. These bricks were graded as best, seconds or thirds in quality, and 'specials' were catered for in the form of splayed bricks, plinth bricks, and 'saddle back' brick copings. Rubbed bricks, so called because they could be rubbed to shape on site, were supplied to form tapered bricks suitable for the curved geometry of brick arches. All in all, this multitude of components would meet the needs of the 1840s building programme and beyond, which when completed would have drastically altered the face of Southampton.

SOUTH WESTERN HOUSE
Formerly the South Western Hotel. This flamboyant edifice epitomizes of the Victorian love of decorative elements in their buildings.

ROYAL SOUTH HANTS HOSPITAL
Built in 1838 and onwards as the Royal South Hants and Southampton Hospital after a small accident hospital on the site.

A few examples of the use of Beaulieu bricks can be cited: firstly the Ordnance Survey Offices in London Road, and the Director General's Office built in 1841. In 1838 construction began on the **Royal South Hants Hospital** in Fanshawe Street using a combination of reds and whites to form an interesting and civilised-looking building, although it has now been altered by many additions around. Nearby **St Andrew's Church** and the **Lamb Memorial Hall** in Brunswick Place, constructed in 1852-3 (now demolished), were built entirely in Beaulieu whites, with stone dressings to both the tower and all openings.

Other materials associated with the Victorian era emerged in Southampton, for instance, the use of cast iron for balconies, railings, and grilles. Cast iron was also used in connection with pavement lights, incorporating glass prism lenses to bend light in order to direct illumination into basement areas, an interesting example of which can be seen in the old kitchen basement of the South Western Hotel (now South Western House). A complete cast-iron structure once existed on the Royal Pier in Victorian times, but alas this beautifully ornate structure has been lost to a fire.

PAINTING AND COLOUR

The Victorians were very colour conscious and delighted in the use of paint as well as all decorative elements to enhance a building. Lead-based paints, manufactured from white lead mixed with turpentine and linseed oil, were the main instruments for decoration, and were used on woodwork as well as plaster walls and ceilings. White lead, the main ingredient (quite toxic in use), was manufactured by suspending sheets of lead above vats of vinegar, the corroded surface of which produced the white lead powder. Pigments were added to create colours, the brightest of which, e.g. red, was the most expensive and therefore reserved for important locations and rooms which did not receive sufficient natural daylight or sunlight. The most common colour for external paintwork of joinery was untinted white lead, which soon assumed an off-white appearance, quite unlike the high gloss of modern paint. Roman cement or lime rendered walls were painted in stone colours, i.e. grey for Portland stone and light yellow (cream) for Bath stone. Rendered walls were also sometimes lined out to simulate joints in stonework, but care was needed when decorating so as not to fill the 'incisions' with paint, thereby negating the effect. Green, cream and browns were common, popular and economical colours to use in Victorian time. Dark green was a favourite for garden railings, known as 'invisible green' when the rails were lost against the green background of the foliage.

SOCIAL COMMENTARY

The Victorian era was typified by the need to achieve detail and decoration as an integral part of the appearance of a building, an art which had its romantic origins in the 19th century Arts and Crafts Movement, which looked back to an era long-gone of rural tranquillity and isolation. There was, of course, a

BRICKWORK AT ST DENYS CHURCH (left and previous page)
Built in 1868 to the designs of Sir George Gilbert-Scott, this church has an interior of mellow red brickwork with some hauntingly beautiful carved figures.

CHRIST CHURCH, HIGHFIELD (right)
It was originally designed by J. A. and R. Brandon in 1846-7. It is a picturesque church in the suburbs now situated between the University to the north and the Collin's Highfield Estate to the south and west.

down side to all this, when we see the artisans' dwellings of the Victorian era, the 'two up and two down' roomed terraces in which people were forced to live close together, within walking distance of their work. This in turn resulted in unhealthy living conditions; the separate zoning of residential areas and industry was absent and the working classes could not move out to the suburbs to live. Sometimes the only escape from this, for the menfolk at least, was to join the armies of Queen Victoria, to go out and police the vast British Empire of that time, and, on occasions, to fight wars for its preservation.

Notwithstanding all this, the face of Southampton changed; the stuccoed terraces of Queens Terrace and curving Oxford Street, reminiscent in appearance of the spa era, came in the early to mid 19th century (on land owned by Queen's College, Oxford). Carlton Crescent (1830s) and a little later Rockstone Place, were built in a similar vein: elegant town houses for the well-to-do, while in the suburbs villas sprang up, as did the consolidation of suburbia, reaching the outer boundaries of the present-day city. Within these districts the Victorians built new churches, or extended those which existed, to serve an expanding population, as follows: in the West, Christ Church, Freemantle (1865-6), Holy Trinity, Millbrook (1873-80) and

St James, Shirley (1836); in the North, St Michael and All Angels, Bassett (1897-1910), Christ Church, Highfield (1846-7), St Denys, St Denys Road (1868), Avenue Congregational Church (1897-8); in the East, Holy Saviour, Bitterne (1852), Peartree Congregational Church (1838), St Mary, Sholing (1866-7), Holy Trinity, Weston (1865), St Mark, Woolston (1863) and Presbyterian Church, Woolston (1876); inner Southampton, St Mary (1878-84, now rebuilt in part after war damage), St Augustine, Northam (1881-4), St Edmund, The Avenue (1889), St Joseph, Bugle Street (1843), St. Luke, Onslow Road (1852-3 now a Sikh temple), St Mark, Archers

HOLY SAVIOUR CHURCH.
This triple-gabled church built in Bitterne village in 1852 and designed by G. Guillaume has high slate roofs and is dominated by a soaring landmark spire.

Road (1890-1, demolished), St Matthew, St Marys Road. (1870), St Peter, Commercial Road (1845-6 redundant – and now in commercial use), United Presbyterian and Congregational Church – St Andrew's, Brunswick Place (1852-3, demolished). This represents a remarkable list of churches built between 1836 and the end of the century, St James, Shirley, being the earliest and St Michael and All Angels, Bassett the last (although it was not completed until 1910, work had begun before the end

ST JAMES, SHIRLEY
A 'commissioners' church designed by W. Hinves in 1836. This yellow brick edifice, with its powerful square tower, now stands in built-up suburbs and faces an area of green parkland to the west.

of the 19th Century, in 1897). At the same time as all this was going on, schools were being built, as were libraries, in pursuit of a better, universal education. Together these edifices represent the seemingly evangelical zeal of the Victorians to cater for both the souls and the minds of the people, although the concept of an egalitarian society *per se* was still a distant horizon.

PEAR TREE GREEN circa 1850.
Engraving by Philip Brannon showing Jesus Chapel commonly called Pear Tree Church. The pear tree that gave its name was possibly planted by Queen Elizabeth I on visiting the town in 1569.
(Reproduced by courtesy of Lawrence Oxley from 'Picture of Southampton')

7. OPEN SPACES

Southampton is blessed with a seascape to the south, framed to the west by the River Test and penetrated to the east by the River Itchen, while inside the city boundaries there are fine open spaces comprising the Common (and cemetery) and the parks. These green areas provide the backdrop to the city's buildings and have been the subject of much comment over the centuries. Southampton at first seems to have no particular form because of the meandering of these inter-connecting vistas of green foliage and floorscape. An unknown writer in 1919 nostalgically returning from the war said 'a peculiarity is that it is difficult to obtain an impression of Southampton as a whole, or comprehend its ramifications at a glance, indeed there are only two methods by which such a perspective can be gained. One is from the Navigation Bridge of a great Atlantic Liner, and the other from the vantage point of the Itchen at Peartree Green.'

SOUTHAMPTON COMMON

Southampton Common with its majestic Avenue, is the first large space seen on entering the city from the north, and was once described as 'one of the greatest ornaments of the town' (Philip Brannon, 1850). In J.B. Priestly's *English Journey* of 1933 he describes the Avenue as 'this fine approach, very gradual and artful in its progression from country to town'. The Common itself extends to some 376 acres (152.16 hectares) of rolling landscape and trees, interspersed with water features, e.g. the cemetery lake (now a wildlife sanctuary). The very few buildings include Holly Lodge, the Cowherds Inn, the Urban Wildlife Centre on the site of the Hawthorns, and the three chapels inside **Southampton Cemetery**. The cemetery itself originally comprised 15 acres (6.07 hectares) of land, was laid out during the period 1845-1863 and landscaped by W.H. Rogers. It was consecrated on the 9th May 1846. Today it is designated as a Site of Special Scientific Interest and is also

CARVED STONE MASK on the entrance gates to the cemetery.

Beneath whose rugged Elms, that Yew-Tree's Shade,
Where heaves the Turf in many a mould'ring Heap,
Each in his narrow Cell for ever laid,
The rude Forefathers of the Hamlet sleep.

(Thomas Gray 1716-1761)

important historically as a record of the people of Southampton. The three chapels erected inside the boundaries, marked by fine stone walls and iron gates, were for the Church of England, the Nonconformists and the Jews. It is recorded that General Juan Manuel de Rosas, a dictator of Argentina who lived in Rockstone House in Carlton Crescent and later Burgess Street Farm, Swaythling, was buried here after his death in 1877. He was by all accounts a flamboyant and enigmatic figure emulated the aura of a man who had known more auspicious times. De Rosas lived out his years in exile in Southampton, after having been plucked from the clutches of a potential lynch mob in 1852, after 17 years of ruthless rule, and carried to England by HMS *Locust*. However, the story does not end here, for in September 1989 his remains were exhumed and returned to Argentina. He now lies in the Recoleta Cemetery in Buenos Aires, having been afforded a full-scale civic funeral by President Carlos Saul Menem.

SOUTHAMPTON COMMON CEMETERY
First laid out during the period 1845-63 by W.H. Rogers, it is now a Site of Special Scientific Interest.

THE COWHERDS

Cattle kept on the Common by the commoners were looked after by the town cowherd who lived in a house built in 1624, during the reign of James I. This property was rebuilt in 1762 and the annual rent increased from £1 to £6 per annum, causing the cowherd to supplement his income by selling beer. Subsequently in 1774 a brewer was appointed as a cowherd, and in 1789, when King George III was on the throne, the house was leased as an inn. Nearby to the Cowherds Inn is the site of the **Hawthorns**, which was both a house and an adjoining brick kiln between 1697 and 1712, until it was pulled down in 1814 and Hawthorn Cottage built in its place. This site was the location of Chipperfields Zoological Gardens between 1961 and 1984; it is now the setting for the Hawthorns Urban Wildlife Centre.

At the north end of the Common lies the **Cutthorn Enclosure**, deriving its name from the practice of holding courts in the open air around a tree or similar feature; the ceremony itself would have dealt with local problems. Other features which no longer exist include the town racecourse opened in 1822, which incorporated a stand for race meetings and followed a chequered career until the last race was run in 1881. (The layout of this course is clearly shown on 'A Complete and Correct Map of Southampton', published by Philip Brannon in 1850.)

An **Artesian Well** was sunk in 1835 to a depth of 1317 feet (401.42 metres), but was abandoned because of insufficient capacity to supply the town's water needs, although the well head position is marked today. In medieval times some of the water supply to the town had originated from a site in Hill Lane which, according to the Reverend Silvester Davies, was called *Conduit Hede* and was connected by a leaden pipe to **Conduit House** in Commercial Road. This was the first recorded piped water supply system in the country, and was subsequently extended to serve developments in Grosvenor Square and the Polygon. Around 1310-11 the friars,

SOUTHAMPTON COMMON about 1850
From an engraving by Philip Brannon. A quintessential idyllic view incorporating a picture of the Cowherds. (Reproduced by courtesy of Lawrence Oxley from 'Picture of Southampton')

who originally controlled the Hill Lane supply, granted to the town water also from the Friary Wall (to the east side of the medieval walled town) to serve English Street, i.e. the High Street. Ultimately the Town Council took over these and other similarly 'owned' installations elsewhere because, as Davies says, the system had '*fallen into decay*'.

Today the Common still retains its grandeur and presence, and in spite of the pressures of modern traffic on the Avenue, is still worthy of Priestly's accolade of 'this fine approach'. In town planning terms, its effect as an introduction to a large vibrant city, which the 'town' has now become, cannot be overstated. It is an element of our heritage which should be protected for all times.

THE PARKS

Moving further southwards, the Inner Avenue is reached, passing the site of Stag Gates and London Road (previously Bellevue Place). The parks of West and East Marlands, incorporating Watts, Andrews and Palmerston Parks, are reached, leading down to Houndwell and Hoglands Parks, which collectively in 1850 were described by Philip Brannon as an '*arboretum*'. These spaces are the heart and lungs of the city and run alongside and parallel to Above Bar Street north to south, and east to west of the north side of the present Civic Centre site. The parks, now designated as areas of 'Special Historic Interest', are also a display of municipal pride, as witnessed by the various memorials to famous people and events. One such event is the sinking of the 'unsinkable' *Titanic*, a ship of the White Star Line which sailed from Southampton on her maiden voyage on Wednesday 10 April 1912, and hit an iceberg and sank on the following Monday 15 April, with the loss of around 1500 lives. Many families in Southampton were affected by this tragedy and there are several memorials to this event, the largest of these is almost opposite the Cenotaph and bears the inscription 'to the memory of the engineer officers of the RMS Titanic who showed their high conception of duty and their heroism by remaining at their posts 15 April 1912.'

The *Cenotaph* itself was designed by Sir Edwin Lutchens in 1919, who also designed the Cenotaph in Whitehall, and is a tall, cambered structure in Portland stone displaying the names of those who fell in the First World War. (Strangely, there are no inscriptions recording those who died in the Second World War.)

Image set
Among sticky buds:

Dated, the marble
Establishes a prodigal
Home for good.

Clear through traffic,
Trains and horns
The Civic Centre chimes
'Our God our help...'

(Jeremy Hooker)

Poem reproduced with the kind permission of Professor Jeremy Hooker.

STATUTE OF ISAAC WATTS IN WATTS PARK among the chestnut trees and seen against the backdrop of the Civic Centre.

These memorials, jointly with the plaque at the Bargate commemorating the litany of the Second World War air raids on Southampton, are an ever-present reminder of the various periods of tragedy borne by the people of this town during the course of the 20th century.

Standing in West Marlands, now called **Watts Park**, on previously common land which was probably laid out as a park in the period 1850-60, is the statue of Isaac Watts (1674-1748). The best known of this writer's sermons, poems and hymns is, 'Our God Our Help in Ages Past' set to a tune now played by the bells of the Civic Centre clock tower. Today the Isaac Watts Memorial Church stands in Winchester Road, although the Watts family had originally been persecuted for their Nonconformist religious beliefs, such are 'the stings and arrows of outrageous fortune.'

The character of these parks changes with the seasons, best marked by the growth pattern of the horse-chestnut trees, *Aesculus hippocastanum*, in Watts Park, from the bare branches of the majestic canopies during winter to the bursting of the leaf buds in spring, and from the luxurious foliage of the summer to the harvest of horse-chestnuts, or 'conkers', on the ground in the autumn. One must also remember the displays of spring crocuses and daffodils followed by the emerging colour in the municipal flower-beds in the summer, seen against the backdrop of the foliage of ground cover and bushes.

It is against this horticultural scene, well described by Philip Brannon as our 'Arboretum', that we view the perspectives of the city's buildings. Sadly, as this book is being written, one of the finest landmark buildings seen from these parks is fast disappearing from view, victim of the process of demolition; namely the **Church of St Andrew** in Brunswick Place. The fine tower, resplendent in Beaulieu white bricks and stone dressings, designed in the Gothic style of the so-called Commissioners Churches of the 19th century, had however achieved a state of terminal decline, having already 'died' as a result of redundancy and subsequent vandalism. Finding a viable alternative use for this architectural dinosaur was thwarted at every stage by restoration costs soaring out of control. Again the words of the Reverend R. Warner come to mind on the subject of buildings which, like men, 'have all their determined periods of decay, beyond which their duration cannot be extended'.

THE RIVERS

The next two most significant open spaces are the river corridors of the Itchen and the Test, each with its individual and idiosyncratic characteristics. The **River Itchen** is of considerable significance, forming a meandering corridor of water and space, having a large area of Southampton on its eastern shore, including the site of Roman Clausentum. It is for this reason that the three main road bridges (and railway) which span this river are so important. Near the mouth of the river is the 'new' **Itchen Bridge** inaugurated in 1974; it follows a course both parallel and adjacent to the old floating bridge. Engineers Travers Morgan & Partners were responsible for the design of this imposing, reinforced concrete structure which took three years to build. It has a central span of some 350 feet (106.68 metres) and provision for a 'headroom' of 80 feet (24.38 metres) above high water spring tides over a width of 100 feet (30.48 metres), Seen from the Woolston Shore, it presents a fine visual display of geometry and engineering, and beneath its long, slender arches is framed a panoramic view of Southampton on the far shore, with the spire of St Mary's Church pointing to the site of Saxon Hamwic.

Immediately to the south of the bridge are the remains of the slipways which served the old floating bridge, immortalised in a painting by Lawrence S. Lowry. This artist captured the scenes of the northern industrial landscape brilliantly, painting from his home in Salford, Lancashire, until his death in 1976. In this picture entitled *The Floating Bridge, Southampton* the human figures crowded on to the decks of the bridge look passively on, entrapped by this product of the machine age in a sort of eerie silence, so typical of the artist's style.

When the **Itchen Floating Bridge** was opened on 23 November 1836, 'the Committee, Proprietors and Officers of the Company' assembled in the morning at the Star Inn, prior to the ceremony at midday, and dined afterwards for the princely sum of twelve shillings and sixpence. This bridge, designed by J.M. Rendel, was encouragingly described at the time as 'the neatest and most commodious boat passage in Europe', and by all accounts the journey was as much a social affair, with refreshments served on board. However, the project was destined at first to run into serious financial problems in its commercial operation, as it was unable to compete with the toll levels of the Northam Road Bridge to the north. The floating bridge had a chequered history until finally it was replaced by the new road bridge, but to anyone who has in the past travelled on this creaking, chain-driven contraption, it had a sort of magic not emulated by more sophisticated modes of travel.

The FLOATING BRIDGE at Woolston. (Reproduced by courtesy of The Francis Frith Collection)

Sailing northwards, as it were, upstream and immediately to the right is the open space of **Peartree Green**, perched high on the river bank and acting host there to **Jesus Chapel**. Consecrated in 1620, this is thought to be the first church built in England after the Reformation although it was subsequently altered. This part of Southampton, originally in the Parish of St Mary (called St Mary Extra), was not very conveniently placed to visit the Mother Church. It involved a hazardous journey by ferry boat and an often uncomfortable wait in Cross House Shelter for the boat to arrive. One 'Richard Smith Esquire' provided the sum of £500 to build this church, some stones of which came from the Roman camp at Clausentum. The church today stands in splendid isolation to the north-east corner of Peartree Green with an iron railing fence surrounding the churchyard, which certainly gives an ageless aura to its green setting.

Just further north at **Freemantle Common**, traces of the old Roman Road leading from Clausentum to *Novio Magus* exist. A plaque here records the line of this road, route 421 from Chichester to Bitterne, 'proved by excavations'. Just south of Clausentum itself is the present **Northam Bridge**, opened in 1954 and designed by Messrs Rendel, Palmer and Tritton, Consultant Engineers. In pre-stressed concrete 'with gleaming bronze railings', it replaces the original wrought-iron bridge dating from 1889. Prior to this in 1796 a timber-framed bridge was built in this location on timber piles, as seen in an 1850 engraving by Philip Brannon.

COBDEN BRIDGE
Named after Richard Cobden, a liberal reformer for 'free use of the inhabitants forever'

The bridge is shown set in a sylvan landscape with Clausentum in the background and the Northam shore in the foreground, complete with sailing ships at the quayside!

The grey stone bridge at **Cobden** (opened in 1928) links St Denys on the west bank with Bitterne on the east, to replace the original bridge of 1883. The five elliptic arches, buttresses and parapet present a handsome appearance when viewed from the river bank.

WOODMILL

The river proceeds further north, until Woodmill where the tidal waters end and the fresh water streams begin, once famous for Woodmill salmon. There has probably been a mill on this site since Saxon times, and over the centuries the grinding of corn was carried on here. The Woodmill Salmon Fishery nearby today was first established by monks in the 9th century 'as a ready made larder' and features in the Domesday Book, for generations it was the property of Lord Swaythling. Nearby are the grounds of **South Stoneham House**, laid out by Lancelot Brown, with the house itself designed by Nicholas Hawksmoor and built in 1708 in the reign of Queen Anne. This red brick edifice has a fine staircase inside, but has been altered externally with the addition of side wings. Still in the same orbit is found **South Stoneham Church**; immediately adjacent to both Stoneham House and Woodmill, it is small, almost gemlike because of its size, but nevertheless important architecturally, and is found in a sylvan setting of trees with the river nearby. The east chancel is 12th century and the font in the nave is of the same date. The nave itself dates from the 13th century, although its windows were reconstructed in the 19th century. The east window is in the perpendicular gothic style of the 15th century, while the tower at the west end is of a similar period. A sun-dial high up on the south face of this tower bears the inscription 'So life flies

MANSBRIDGE
This single arch, 18th century stone bridge was the earliest and first crossing place at the River Itchen before the construction of later bridges to the south.

away'. A Coverdale Bible of 1572 is one of this church's important treasures. Reference has been made to the bridge at **Mansbridge** – a stone, single arch affair which in the late 18th century was the first and only crossing point of the river for traffic. Today it stands in isolation with a new bridge to take away the heavy traffic. It is linked along the river path to the nearby White Swan Inn. Although much modernised and extended, this inn has nevertheless retained in essence the character of what was once just a cottage.

TOWNHILL PARK HOUSE

Townhill Park House, once the home of Lord and Lady Swaythling, comprises an original villa on the site (*circa* 1795), with early 20th century wings added by the architect L. Rome Guthrie. Construction of these wings was started in 1910 and completed in two stages after a delay resulting from the First World War. The plan of the resultant house is L-shaped with formal gardens to the north-west and a kitchen garden with outbuildings, including a fine two-storey stable block, to the south-east. Both house and grounds enjoy an elevated position above the Itchen Valley, located on the extremity of the city boundary and today in fairly close proximity to both the M27 motorway and Southampton (Eastleigh) Airport.

The design of the house is essentially in the Palladian manner, with rendered elevations incorporating sash-windows beneath a tiled roof, and a projecting arched portico and pediment to the front entrance. Inside there are some fine panelled rooms, in particular the Music Room and the so-called 'Boudoir' used by Lady Swaythling as a reception room; the panelling referred to originally came from Chantry House in Nottinghamshire.

A major feature of the grounds comprised a sunken garden and herb garden facing the terraces of the north-west front, complete with an extended pergola feature and tiled roof to a loggia at the end of the garden vista. This garden is very much in the character of the Arts and Crafts Movement of the late 19th century and early 20th century, and is in style reminiscent of the designs in a book first

TOWNHILL PARK HOUSE, once the home of Lord and Lady Swaythling. Photograph by Peter Kilby.

published in 1912 entitled *Gardens for Small Country Houses* by Gertrude Jekyll and Lawrence Weaver. Gertrude Jekyll, who lived from 1843 until 1932, trained as an artist and then turned her attention to gardens, enjoying a high reputation on the subject, because of both her writings and her collaboration with Edwin Lutchens, the doyen of country house design and architect of that period.

This house, together with South Stoneham House, represent the primary examples in the Southampton environs of the so-called 'country house'. Although they are both originally from different eras, i.e. the early 20th century and 18th century respectively, these houses are nevertheless significant examples of their day in both architectural and landscaping terms.

RIVER TEST

Where the A36 crosses the River Test at Redbridge on the 'modern' causeway built in 1930, there is a spectacular view of the meeting of the reed beds to the north and the open waters of the Test Estuary facing Southampton Docks to the south. Alongside this causeway and at a much lower level, can be seen two old bridges built in stone, the first with a single arch span, the second resplendent with five arches, and interconnected by a short gravel road. It was along this lower road that traffic once travelled to the **Village of Redbridge**, once called *Vadum Arundinis*. This crossing place at the head of the Test Estuary was later known as *Reedford*, its name meaning literally 'a ford through reeds'. This was once the site of a small port, exporting timber and grain and importing coal, and in the 17th century continuing into the 18th century it was a centre for shipbuilding.

The reed beds *(Phragmites communis)* extending over about 75 acres (30.35 hectares), are a magnificent sight, especially when the tide is high and the sunlight glistens upon the water, forming reflections of reeds and the arches of the stone bridges. Two rivers converge here in fact: the smaller Blackwater meets the

REED BEDS AT REDBRIDGE CAUSEWAY
This spot marks the ancient river crossing of the Test at Redbridge once called VADUM ARUNDINIS or REED-FORD and referred to by the Venerable Bede in ad731 by its Saxon name of HREUTFORD.
Photograph by Peter Kilby.

THE OLD ROAD BRIDGES AT REDBRIDGE CAUSEWAY.
Photograph by Peter Kilby.

mainstream of the Test around Nursling to the north, and thereafter the Test continues alone across 420 acres (169.97 hectares) of nature reserve. Managed by the Barker Mill Estate and cared for by the Hampshire Wildlife Trust, this area has been described as 'one of the most important wet lands on the South Coast'.

ENGRAVING OF VADUM ARUNDINIS
Once here were 'the best shipps built'.

At the northern end of the reserve stands the 18th century **Nursling Mill**, built on a frame of beech logs donated in 1728 by Sir Richard Mill. Because of the nature of the terrain, once called these 'spongy water meadows', the river valley at this lower point is a major migration path for birds. One of the finest spectacles in the dying light of a winter sunset is to see literally thousands of starlings swooping and weaving in formation before darkness finally descends and they settle for roosting through the night beneath the arches of the causeway.

The five arch bridge is the earliest of the two, having been rebuilt after its destruction by Royalist forces in 1643, while the single span bridge was added to form a causeway in 1793. This arrangement is well illustrated on a print by G.F. Sargent in 1838.

Because of its proximity to the New Forest, shipbuilding was a major industry, as was the exporting of timber to the shipyards of Portsmouth. One Thomas Nicholls of Redbridge, described as 'Purveyor of the New Forest', carried on a business here, and in the late 18th century pioneered the idea of the economical use of timber in shipbuilding. It was Samuel Bentham (1757-1831) who in 1795 was given permission by the admiralty to construct experimental ships in which he introduced watertanks instead of stone ballast, as well as interior bulkheads and partitions. By 1799 he had built the *Redbridge* (150 tons and 16 guns) and the *Millbrook* (140 tons and 14 guns) described as 'wonderful sea boats, sailing very swiftly'. It was during the same period that ships were launched at Bucklers Hard on the Beaulieu River by Henry Adams, starting in 1749 with the *Mermaid* of 24 guns, and finishing in

THE SINGLE SPAN STONE ARCH BRIDGE AT REDBRIDGE
Photograph by Peter Kilby.

1810 with the last warship *Vengeur* of 74 guns. (Nelson's ship, the *Agamemnon*, 64 guns, was launched here in 1781.) Thus it was that the waters around the Solent were a hive of activity from the mid 18th century to the beginning of the 19th century, building the so-called 'wooden walls of England'. However we read of earlier progress in shipbuilding in the diary of Celia Fiennes who, travelling on horseback throughout the country 'for the sake of her health' in 1695, wrote 'At Portsmouth is a good dock for building shipps, but about six miles off at Bursledon and at Redbridge are the best shipps built'!

The old bridge itself now stops short of Test Lane, leaving room for the railway to pass under the overhead causeway, but providing nevertheless an end-on view of a group of 18th century buildings comprising the **Anchor Hotel** and Nos 63 and 65, formerly outbuildings of the hotel itself. Travelling south beneath the causeway and into Old Redbridge Road, we see **Ivy House**, built in two stages in the 17th and 18th centuries. The main house has a colourwashed brick facade, sash-windows and a tiled roof, together with a nautical-type bay window on its side, facing the original view to the water. There is a medieval timber-framed section to the rear, with several important archaeological artefacts in what was probably once a warehouse section of the building. On the same side of the road next door is the **Ship Inn**, a 16th-17th century brick-facaded building with bow and sash-windows and tiled roof, concealing from view a timber-framed interior, brick fireplaces and ovens to be revealed once inside. Although now hemmed in by modern developments, these buildings hark back to the maritime past and history of this place, as do other remaining 18th and 19th century houses in the road. The whole village is now encapsulated in a sort of happy backwater, bypassed by modern traffic which is nevertheless close at hand but at a seemingly safe distance.

After passing Redbridge, the River Test opens to the wide expanses of water alongside the container terminals of Southampton Docks, Town Quay and the Red Funnel Terminal, and past also the great Ocean Dock and Empress Dock, until the waters of the River Itchen meet, in confluence. Both rivers join forces here to lead into Southampton Water and the Solent beyond. It is from the perspective of the Redbridge Causeway that the full scale of this scene can be appreciated, and the full impact also of Southampton's maritime history, past and present, can best be mused upon from this landward vantage point.

8. THE INTER-WAR YEARS

Following the end of the Great War on Armistice Day 1918, and before the beginning of the Second World War in 1939, the two most significant developments in Southampton (the University excepted) were achieved: the building of the Civic Centre complex between 1928 and 1939, and the emergence of the housing estates in Highfield and Swaythling, designed by the architect Herbert Collins, from 1922 until the onset of war in 1939. Both projects had significant social consequences; the Civic Centre was the manifestation of both municipal pride and the organisation of local government within a custom-built, centralised complex, while the 'Collins Estates' were a demonstration of the best design qualities of the Garden Suburbs. Fashionable at the time, they were built at affordable prices for both sale and letting. Although both examples are dissimilar architecturally, individually they contributed to the civilisation of the way in which people were organised and housed, and both possessed the common thread of fitting admirably into their respective settings.

CIVIC CENTRE

Designs for the new Civic Centre building were prepared by the architect E. Berry Webber in 1928, and work started on the foundations for the Municipal Block in the same year. The building which we see today was built in four stages, namely the Municipal Block completed in 1932, the Law Courts and Clock Tower completed in 1933, while the Guildhall was finished in 1937, and finally the Art Block (incorporating the Art Gallery, Art School and Library) was opened in 1939, just before the outbreak of war. The phasing of the building is significant and is reflected in the overall plan form of the completed scheme, with each of the four elements expressed and interconnected by link blocks. The internal character of each part changes with the varying functions; the common denominator is seen in the unifying consistency of the linking through of the public spaces inside. Outside there is an overall symmetry and unity of design, although the siting of the Clock Tower to one side introduces an overtone of asymmetry and contrast to the balance of the composition.

The building has been described by Pevsner Lloyd as 'perhaps the most ambitious civic building erected in the provinces in the inter-war years, a symbol of Southampton's heyday as a port, prospering while the rest of the country was in the darkness of slump'. There is a cross fall on the site overall, creating the entrance of the Municipal Block to the South a monumental stone staircase up to the main entrance (providing difficult access for the disabled by today's standards), while at the far north side the Library Block access is at median

BERRY WEBBER'S ORIGINAL COMPETITION-WINNING DESIGNS FOR THE CIVIC CENTRE (1928). Taken from photographs held by Southampton Archives Services. By courtesy of Berry Webber and Partners (incorporated with AHP Partnership on 1.1.96)

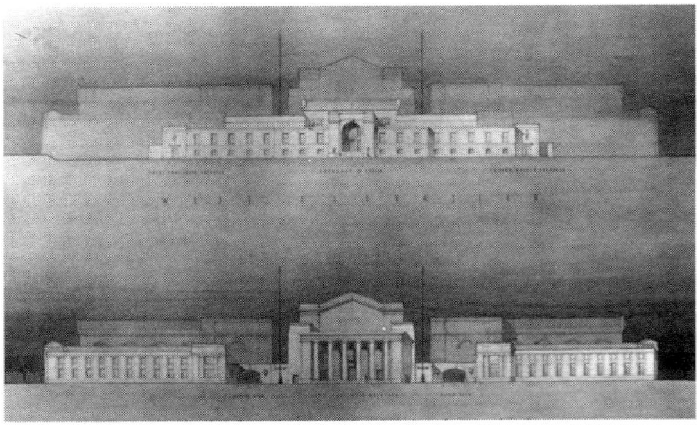

level. The land on which the complex stands is part of the medieval fields around the city centre called West Marlands, a derivative of 'Magdalens' which is land traditionally related to Lammas, the first of August formerly observed as Harvest Festival by the Church.

The building itself is a steel-framed structure, with an external envelope of fine dressed Portland stone ashlar, built against a brick inner skin. Windows generally are steel casements and the main doors finely are grained hardwood. Where pitched roofs occur they are clad in copper, giving that fine green patina of age when exposed to the elements over a number of years, but also causing some anxiety where the green staining has adversely affected stone dressings, particularly on the Clock Tower to the Law Courts.

Architecturally there is a classical formality about the external appearance, with the dominance of solid over void, i.e. walls to windows, creating a sense of solidity and timelessness. Around the building we see fine, grey cobbled stone surfaces on the roads and forecourts of the Municipal Block to the south and the Guildhall to the east, combined with smooth, running surfaces of blue brick paviors for ease of movement. Around these open areas there are some fine, low walls, again in dressed Portland stone, with smooth, curved copings defining both the vehicular and pedestrian surfaces and also enclosing some immaculately-kept lawns.

When the various buildings of the Civic Centre were opened, there were of course official ceremonies to mark these events. The most auspicious of these was the first when, on Tuesday 5 November 1932, the then Duke and Duchess of York opened the Municipal Block. The official programme of this event records that the royal visitors arrived at Southampton by train (at Blechynden Terrace) to be greeted by the Lord Lieutenant of Hampshire. In order to alert a waiting mayor and other dignitaries at the Civic Centre, a 'maroon' was fired to indicate their departure

MAYOR'S RECEPTION ROOM
A room of some considerable grandeur and presence.

MAYOR'S CORRIDOR/SUITE
Resplendent with the mural taken from the dining saloon of the liner QUEEN ELIZABETH.

from the station. At the Civic Centre entrance the architect, Mr Berry Webber, presented a key to the royal visitors who were then requested to open the door, and inside afterwards the building was dedicated by the Bishop of Winchester with the words 'to the glory of God and for the service of this ancient town we dedicate this building'. Following the unveiling of the foundation stone ceremony the royal party departed to take 'luncheon' at the South Western Hotel. Afterwards the Duke and Duchess made an official inspection of the New Docks extension works and the Graving Dock, which was under construction (later the King George V Dry Dock). Such was the importance of the events and activities of the city and port at that time, that personages no less than the future king and his consort graced that day with their presence.

What then did the first visitors to this new building see and experience? Firstly they saw an interior much as it is today, a great entrance hall with marble floor leading to a double flight stone staircase with beautifully carved stone balusters, all surmounted by an ornate coffred ceiling. The Council Chamber which was entered from the head of this staircase via leather-clad and iron-studded sound-proofed doors, leading in turn to the 'horseshoe' seating layout and finely timber-panelled walls and ornate ceiling, on which the points of the compass are marked – a good nautical touch! Outside the Council Chamber again, and on the opposing end of the stairwell and galleried access, is the Mayor's Reception Hall. This is a rather sombre room, where grey Forest of Dean slate is featured extensively, but the overall effect is one of some considerable grandeur and presence. The corridor leading to the Mayor's Suite *today* contains three very interesting wall features, namely:

1. A large mural feature in brown and cream, taken from the dining saloon of the liner *Queen Elizabeth*.
2. A beautiful tapestry commemorating D-Day which once hung in the Guildhall above the Bargate, reminiscent, on a miniature scale, of the famous Bayeux Tapestry depicting the Battle of Hastings.
3. A fine, architect's perspective drawing of the designs for the Civic Centre.

The overall effect of the interior public spaces and committee rooms in the Municipal Block retains the feeling and character of the 1930s, and what we see today is, in essence, the design handed down to this generation, which because of its uniqueness to Southampton, should be nurtured and preserved.

HERBERT COLLINS AND HIS WORK

Anyone wandering into Highfield Close off Brookvale Road, and seeing for the first time the cluster of rendered houses grouped around a courtyard garden with wrought ironwork arches, sunken pond and lush foliage, could be forgiven for thinking that they had arrived at another Portmeirion-type development, a showpiece of village life in Wales originating from the imagination of the architect Clough Williams-Ellis. However, this particular gem was designed in the 1920s by Southampton architect Herbert Collins, in the same era that Clough Williams-Ellis was producing his Portmeirion masterpiece. Both design philosophies share the common ingredient of the masterful fusion of architecture with landscape, producing an almost magical sylvan setting in which to live. Today this atmosphere is reminiscent of a seemingly soporific age, epitomised by carpet slippers and pipe-smoking in front of an open fire, with cocoa at bedtime!

HERBERT COLLINS PLAQUE
Uplands Estate.

Herbert Collins was responsible for the design of two principal estates in the city; firstly the so-called Uplands Estate, incorporating Brookvale Road, Highfield Close, Uplands Way, and Orchards Way, as well as Glebe Court across Highfield Lane. The second such estate, built later, is the Ethelbert Avenue Estate, including Field Close and Leaside Way, off Bassett Green Road. Today both estates have been designated Conservation Areas in recognition of the need to protect their rare qualities. Within these estates houses are essentially to a design which estate agents today would describe as 'cottage style' with beautiful faced brickwork to the walls, timber small-paned casement windows, and plain or roman clay tiled roofs surmounted by brick chimney stacks. Although there are great variations in design within the overall theme, there is a consistent unity of purpose running throughout, down to the control of colours of paintwork, so essential to maintaining the visual unity. Away from the houses nothing has been left to chance: carefully designed brick pavements inside a grassed verge (Orchards Way); provision of a semi-wild open space at the junction of Uplands

HIGHFIELD CLOSE A Portmeirion setting?

Way and Orchards Way, with its stream and fine, mature trees around; a formal open space in the form of a large, sunken grassed area, screened from the road by a vast holly bush *(Ilex aquifolium)* at Glebe Court; and the maintenance of gravelled roads in Glebe Court again and Ethelbert Avenue. Even the post-box has not been overlooked, and is built into its own brick feature in Orchards Way. At every turn we see the hand of the architect at work, and the sureness of his eyes. Although many of these house's interiors have been altered in response to modern living,

ORCHARDS WAY On high embankments, the houses are framed against informal gardens of superb quality.

some remain in their original form, at least in part, for instance 22 Orchards Way is a terraced house on a high embankment, framed against informal gardens of superb quality. The living room and dining room are much as Collins left them, and upstairs there is a vanity unit made of joinery taken, we are told, from a redundant church; recycling is no new thing!

Herbert Collins was an idealist then, and like all such people, appeared to live his life by a set of strong principles, exampled by his work for the League of Nations and United Nations in Southampton. His dream had been to build a garden city,

UPLANDS ESTATE
Today the mature landscaping has a dreamlike quality evoking the comment that HIGHFIELD (in which this estate stands) is a 'state of mind'.

GLEBE COURT screened from the road by a vast holly hedge.

and in this he was greatly influenced by the work of Ebenezer Howard and the Garden City Movement, and in so doing had served on the Board of Directors of Welwyn Garden City. Today the leaseholds of the properties are managed by his heir and daughter, Julie Oswell and further interests are protected by strong and active residents associations. In his definitive work on Herbert Collins, his biographer, architect Robert Williams, describe him as 'Architect and Worker for Peace', a fitting epitaph for anyone.

POSTSCRIPT TO THE INTER-WAR YEARS

On 22 June 1934 at 8.15 p.m., the first film to be screened in the newly completed Regal Cinema in Above Bar Street was *Love, Life and Laughter,* starring Miss Gracie Fields as Nellie. The famous Reginald Foort played the 'Regal Wonder Organ' and in the opening ceremony on that day Gracie Fields and her producer Basil Dean 'graciously consented to make a personal appearance'. This new cinema, built on the site of the Alexandra Theatre had been designed by the architects team of Frank Verity and S. Beverley. The cinema was described at the time as 'not aggressively modern but just sufficiently so to harmonise with any future developments in Above Bar'. Inside the auditorium there was a capacity for 1756 seats in the stalls and balcony, with a fully equipped stage for theatrical productions, in addition to films. At first floor level at the front was the café lounge, with its striking chevron-shaped windows reaching from the floor to the vaulted ceiling. For its day the building was very technically advanced, with projecting equipment

THE ODEON CINEMA
A lost 'monument to the movies'.

described as a 'super simplex mechanism' together with a 'Western Electric Wide Range Sound System'. The building was air-conditioned by plenum ventilation, while the overall lighting scheme throughout employed '5000 osram lamps'. Photographs of this fine building, which was demolished in 1993, show a powerful and imposing structure, very typical of its age in design terms. The horizontal window fenestration slots were counterbalanced by vertical features, in the all-stone elevation above an originally marble-clad entrance storey. This cinema, subsequently called 'the Odeon', was in every respect 'a monument to the movies', harking back to an era before television when magic, or so it seemed, danced upon the silver screen, and we were in our imaginations transported to another place in the world. In its absence from today's street scene this building, with all its memories, will be sorely missed.

9. WORLD WAR II

SOUTHAMPTON: THE SPITFIRE, THE BLITZ AND THE AFTERMATH

In a hangar-like modern building called the 'Hall of Aviation' in Albert Road South, stands among the exhibits a Supermarine Spitfire, call sign PK683. Designed and probably built at the Supermarine Works at Woolston, the Spitfire, brainchild of R.J. Mitchell (1895-1937), was of its age the most deadly fighting machine invented. Mitchell, Supermarine's chief designer, had previously been involved with the success of the Supermarine Rolls-Royce S.6 (winner of the Schneider Trophy in 1929), which subsequently achieved the world speed record of 357.7 m.p.h.

The sequence of events leading to the production of the Spitfire is an interesting one, when initially the Air Ministry of the time issued a specification to Supermarine for a single-seat day or night fighter which, known as Type 224, achieved an air speed of 228 m.p.h., although this was 30 m.p.h. below requirements. Modifications were made to produce the Type 300, with smaller wings, retractable under-carriage and enclosed canopy, powered by a Rolls-Royce PV12 engine (later to be known as the 'Merlin'). This plane, with its unmistakable elliptical-shaped wings, became the pedigree for all that was to follow, namely prototype K.5054, 'built in secret at Woolston and Eastleigh' and flown by test pilot Joseph 'Mutt' Summers on the 5 or 6 March 1936. Subsequently the Air Ministry ordered 310 Spitfires, and the first prototype Mk(1) was delivered to 19 Squadron RAF at Duxford Airfield in Cambridgeshire in August 1938. Sadly Reg Mitchell died of cancer in 1937 therefore never having lived to see the devastating effect of his creation. The fact that this fighter was produced in secret and delivered to the RAF a year before the outbreak of war contradicts the myth that the onset of the

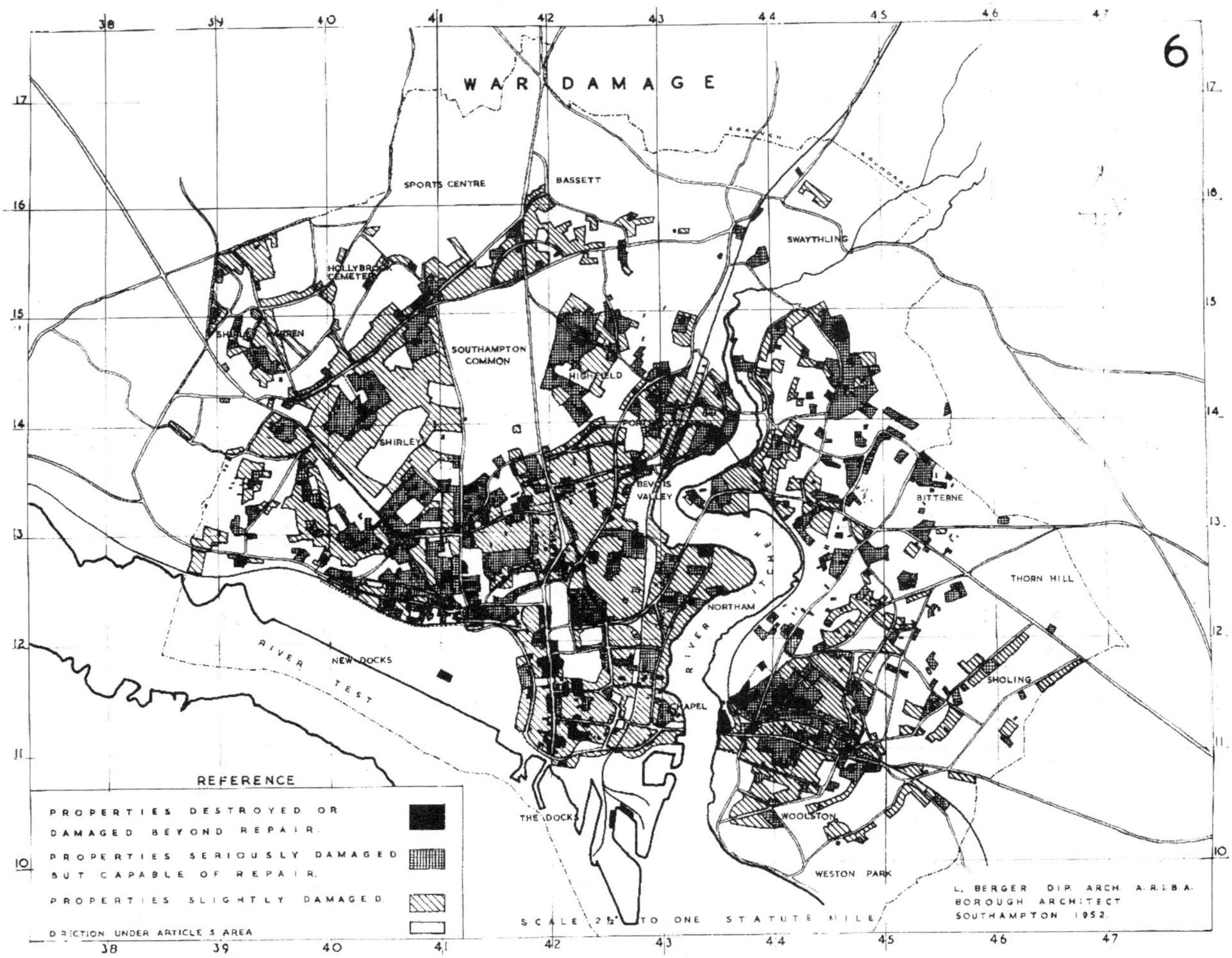

WAR DAMAGE IN SOUTHAMPTON. (Reproduced by courtesy of Ordnance Survey and Southampton Archives Services)

THE SUPERMARINE SPITFIRE
(call sign PK683)
This now stands in the Hall of Aviation, Southampton and is a reminder of 'the most deadly fighting machine' designed by R.J. Mitchell (1895-1937).

war came as a surprise to the government of the day, bearing in mind that plans for the production of this plane were set in progress in the early 1930s. Be that as it may, the Spitfire in conjunction with the Hawker Hurricane, together with their pilots, most certainly turned the so-called Battle of Britain to this country's favour when, in 1940 a bloody and decisive aerial battle was fought above London and the harvest fields of Southern England and over the Channel. On the ground we saw the curving vapour trails of the fighters in combat and heard the gunfire, which heralded the 'kill' when the stricken aircraft spiralled to the ground and oblivion, a manœuvre once described as 'the dance of death'.

In Russell Place, Portswood, a quiet suburb of Southampton, Mitchell's memory is recorded by a small plaque on the garage of the house where he last lived; a modest memorial to a man of some genius, and a dedication to his craft.

THE BLITZ

Almost as an act of retribution, or so it may seem, Southampton, the birthplace of the Spitfire, was singled out for a terrible revenge from the air. Alongside the Bargate in Above Bar a plaque records the air raids which followed between 1940 and 1944. The plaque records the awesome statistics of those years when 631 people were killed and 1888 injured. Also, during this time some 3589 buildings were destroyed and 40,946 damaged. In all, 2631 high-explosive bombs and 30,652 incendiary devices were dropped on the town. A visitor to the town at the height of the Blitz said that an air raid was in progress when his train approached Southampton Central Station, making it necessary to wait in the tunnel until the 'all clear'. On arriving at the station, or what was left of it, he saw outside a scene of devastation 'worse than in London' from where he had just travelled.

It is against this sort of background that we must now judge the appearance of the city today, since the wholesale destruction of both the buildings and the infrastructure will account for much of the 'new' development. In the early 1950s many sites in the city centre were still occupied by temporary shops, although some of the planned reconstruction had already started, as had that of the new housing estates in the suburbs. The city had the overall appearance of a battle-worn community recovering, as it were, from near-fatal wounds. Miraculously, however, much of the significant historic fabric has survived; important buildings like the Bargate and the historic inns of the Star, Dolphin and Red Lion, although blast affected, were still there, as was St Michael's Church and its spire. Often a church spire, and to some extent the Civic Centre clock tower have survived, as they may have been used as markers and navigation aids by the planes attacking the town. Many of the buildings which did survive have until this day carried the scars of latent damage brought about by the blast and shaking of the foundations. This hypothesis is more and more evident as historic buildings in particular are opened up for repair today.

These interesting views of St Marys Church, the mother church of Southampton, show the damaged shell and its reconstruction in 1954-6. Photographs reproduced by courtesy of the Southern Daily Echo.

RECONSTRUCTION AND RECOVERY

As in other towns and cities which were similarly devastated, it was seen in planning circles as an opportunity to provide the perfect master plan for the future. However, shortages of resources in the immediate post-war period would necessarily have affected the manner in which the first steps were taken to effect the rebuilding programme, when the object of the exercise would have been

THE AFTERMATH OF THE WAR - A VIEW OF THE HIGH STREET
A scene of almost total devastation. Reproduced by courtesy of Southampton City Museums.

to obtain the best results with the resources available.

It was during the 1950s and 1960s that architects and designers were looking at ways and means of speeding up the rebuilding process by using industrialised building techniques. A building site is at best a crude sort of open-air factory, put together and organised for each individual contract. Weather plays an important role in this, affecting not only progress but also the quality of the end product. With this in mind, thoughts had turned to the idea of producing components wholesale under controlled factory conditions off-site, and assembling them relatively quickly on-site, as it were. In order to achieve this aim, the components so produced required to be not only suitable for the purpose for which they were designed, but more importantly, to fit on arrival! To this end therefore, a system of modular co-ordination was evolved, in which all components could be identified and set out to a known dimensional grid.

This design ethic obviously had an effect on the appearance of buildings so produced, and accounts in no small degree for the apparent regimentation of form associated with buildings of this era. In addition, the outer skin of these structures of the 1950s and onwards exhibited in many examples the presence of a continuous glass facade, or 'curtain wall', a term derived from the enclosing masonry wall of a medieval castle. However, this design philosophy, based on the assembly of pre-fabricated components, was not new but had germinated from techniques started in the Industrial

VYSE LANE FLATS facing Bugle Street. The old and the new sit gracefully together. Photograph by Peter Kilby.

Revolution in England, and expanded upon in Victorian times, with beautiful effects, especially in the use of cast iron, for both structural work and decorative elements.

Within the confines of the Old Town Conservation Area of Southampton there are examples of this modern building, forming part of a medieval and Victorian setting, namely the **Vyse Lane flats.** Built by Lyons, Israel and Ellis, in 1958 for Southampton Corporation, the flats stand in Castle Way but are visible from Bugle Street and French Street; the fourteen-storey flats of Castle House, were designed by Eric Lyons in 1963. The Vyse Lane flats are three-storey facing on to Bugle Street and four-storey facing French Street behind, built in a box frame technique with yellow facing brick end walls and concrete cross walls and floors; the windows and under sill panels are in green, either on the wall faces or set back in recesses formed by balconies. Framed against the adjacent half-timbered Duke of Wellington Public House, an early 16th century house and shop, these modern flats blend well with their setting in scale, and the way they have been placed down in the street scene.

The **Castle House flats**, built on the site of Southampton Castle Keep, have been designed to relate to the vertical emphasis of the spire of St Michael's Church to the south. The solid purple and blue brick podium on which this concrete- framed structure stands is reminiscent of the solidarity, robustness and monolithic strength of the medieval Town Walls nearby, while the monochrome colour scheme of black and white links with the similar lines of the timber-framed buildings in Bugle Street and French Street.

CASTLE HOUSE (flats in the background)
Built on the site of the Southampton Castle Keep, it is reminiscent of the solidity, robustness and monolithic strength of the medieval town walls nearby. Photograph by Peter Kilby.

Together the Vyse Lane and Castle House flats represent a clear example of the design ethos of the 1950s and 1960s, in which the scale of the setting into which these new buildings have been placed is of paramount importance. The way the designs have responded positively and accurately is a measure of the successful integration of these elements into the street scene, which itself has been subject to continual change over the centuries.

The main areas of redevelopment in the town centre were concentrated in Above Bar, to the north of the Bargate, and in the High Street to the south. The new buildings to the north of the Bargate stand in what was the main shopping area in the 1950s, as it is today, although they now form the background to a pedestrian precinct which has replaced the through road. The buildings have been rebuilt in a generally three-storey configuration of stone-clad buildings, vaguely classical in appearance but with overtones of modernity in the design detail, especially in the case of window openings with fins and slits and the like. Little has changed here today, other than the alterations to shop fronts to suit differing ownerships. There is a general feeling of austerity in this

ABOVE BAR TODAY, now a pedestrian precinct. Photograph by Peter Kilby.

design, and the only suggestion of a hint of luxury at the time, i.e. in the 1950s, was the first-floor dining room of the Cadena Café next door to Boots the Chemist. This café (now closed) had a monochrome interior, reminiscent of the coffee houses of the 1930s, and had a unique character of those days now long passed.

In the **High Street** to the south of the Bargate it is a different story, with new buildings (especially on the west side of the road) built in an unashamedly modern design; forty years or so on they have stood the test of time in retaining the freshness and verve of the time of their conception. Of this street, J.B. Priestley once wrote 'at the bottom of the High Street, you must go carefully, otherwise you may lose England altogether and find yourself looking ... at the Table Mountain'. He was of course alluding to the connection with the ocean liners, (his book was *English Journey*, written in 1934), and Southampton's nearness to the sea and the rest of the world.

It would therefore seem appropriate at this stage to talk about the **Ocean Terminal Building**, built in Southampton in 1950 and described as 'this impressive and beautiful reception station, a new and magnificent entry into Great Britain'. Therefore at a time of austerity, a confident statement of the magnitude of this building for the future of sea travel and cruising, before the advent of universal air travel, was bracing news indeed for Southampton. This fine terminal was opened by the Prime Minister of the time, Clement Attlee, to receive the premier liners of the day, allowing for the berthing of such ships as the *Queen Elizabeth* 83,000 tons

OCEAN TERMINAL AND QUEEN ELIZABETH
(Photograph by courtesy of Associated British Ports)

and 1031 feet long (314.25 metres), the *Queen Mary* 81,000 tons and 1020 feet long (310.89 metres) and the *Mauretania*, 35,000 tons and 771 feet in length (235.00 metres). In the first year of the operation of this terminal, 114 ships used this facility. The building was designed by the architect C.B. Dromgoole, and was constructed with a steel frame and concrete floors, with walls either glazed or in pre-cast concrete panels. The overall structure was three storeys in height with a distinctive semicircular tower at the south end. In the technical press of the day it was described in the *Architect and Building News* as 1272 feet long (387.7 metres) and 111 feet wide (33.8 metres) (against the Queen Elizabeth's length of 1031 feet: 314.24 metres). Telescopic gangways linked the ship with the waiting halls situated at first floor level, baggage handling at ground floor (with direct access to the boat trains), and a viewing gallery on the top deck. In an article in the *Nautical Magazine* of 1950 by Commander J. Radford R.N.R., the building was described as 'strikingly modern' and it goes on to list the facilities to include 'comfortable seating and refreshment buffets, ample telephone kiosks, telegraph and cable offices, bureau de change', etc. Photographs of the interior suggest it to have been a splendid and fitting point of entry to this country, although sadly the terminal was demolished in 1983 amid an outcry of disapproval.

Clement Attlee was also responsible for backing the Festival of Britain, held on London's South Bank in 1951, with memories of Powell and Moya's breathtaking Skylon feature, Ralph Tubb's Dome of Discovery and alongside, the Royal Festival Hall designed by the then London County Council architects R. Matthew and L. Martin. This exhibition sums up the 1950s – in design terms – as an exciting, brave new world, dubbed the era of 'the Skylon, the Pylon and the Nylon'.

10. THE UNIVERSITY OF SOUTHAMPTON AND THE HARTLEY INSTITUTION

At the junction of the High Street and Briton Street, and on a modern ware house building, there is a plaque recording the origins and place of the Hartley Institution and an outline of the intriguing circumstances leading to the founding of the University of Southampton. On this same site originally stood what the Reverend J. Silvester Davies has described in 1883 as 'the three dreary-looking red-brick houses with narrow casements, dating apparently from the early part of the last century, in one of which Henry Robinson Hartley formerly resided, as his father has before him'. Henry Robinson Hartley inherited his father's considerable estate in 1800, based on an import business in the wine trade. In about 1824, however, after a long-standing dispute with an immediate neighbour, he closed his house and left Southampton, never to reside there again. He died in Calais at the age of 72 in the year of 1850, and surprisingly left the bulk of his estate to the mayor and corporation of 'his native town'. Under the terms of this will he bequeathed, for the purpose of the education of a 'select scientific public' to study the sciences of natural history, astronomy, antiquities and classical and Oriental literature in a building which was to contain a public library, botanic gardens, observatory and collections related to the above arts and sciences. The amount of the legacy, although depleted by litigation after the will had been disputed by Hartley's family, still totalled a considerable sum; allowing the staffing, equipping and building of what has been described as 'a handsome palladian structure, on three storeys' facing on to the High Street. (Hartley had lived at No. 65 High Street, on land leased from Queen's College, Oxford). The plan of this building is seen in the 1870 Ordnance Survey map of the area, in which the 'Hartley Institution' is shown on the ground floor to possess a council room, museum and lecture hall

THE HARTLEY INSTITUTE ON ITS OPENING DAY
Reproduced by courtesy of Southampton Archive Services

with an apsidal end, said to seat 1000 people. There is a courtyard garden and walled garden in the complex, leading down to the Back of the Walls where one would have expected to see the 'botanical garden' element. According to the Reverend Silvester Davies these buildings are thought to have cost in the region of £20,000, a substantial sum for the day; the library alone contained some 20,000 volumes. Within this building on the other floors there is note also of a School of Art, a School of Science and Engineering, and what is described as a 'Junior Medical School'. These facilities, together with a department of General Literature, and Chemical and Physical Laboratories among others, were used by students paying between £15 and £24 per annum, while in the years 1881-2 there were 340 students enrolled for both day and evening classes.

The Institution was governed by a council of the mayor and nine members of the Town Council, plus six others. So began the birth of the university of the 19th and 20th centuries and beyond. It is interesting to note the liberalisation of the interpretation of the terms of Hartley's original will, from the concept of 'a select and scientific public' to the inclusion of a 'public library' and provision for 'artisans'' evening classes from the outset.

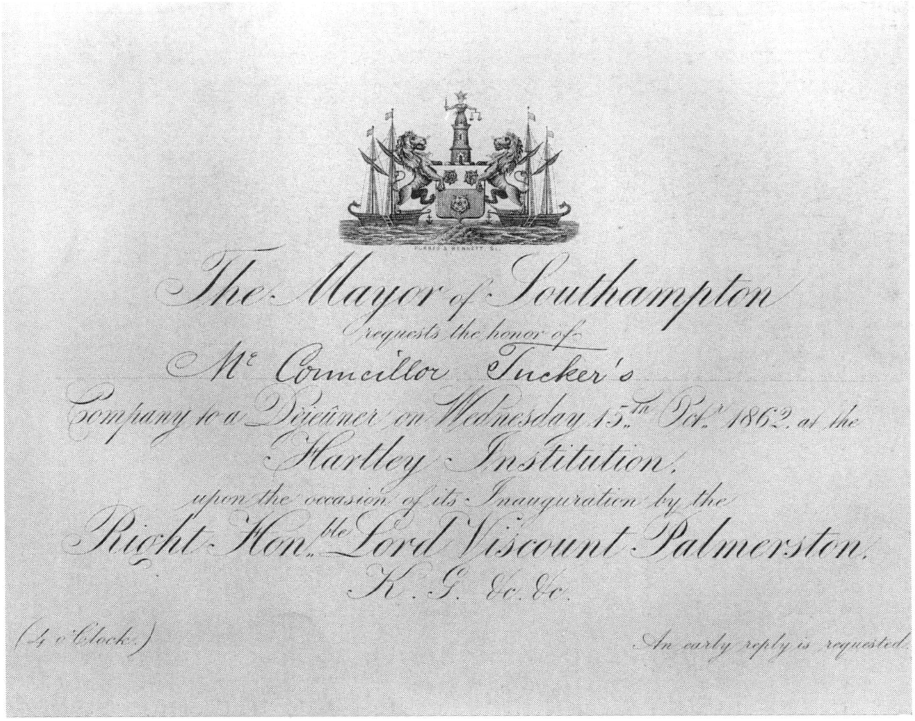
The Mayor of Southampton
requests the honor of
Mr Councillor Tucker's
Company to a Déjeuner on Wednesday 15th Oct. 1862, at the
Hartley Institution,
upon the occasion of its Inauguration by the
Right Honble Lord Viscount Palmerston.
K. G. &c. &c.
(4 o'Clock.)
An early reply is requested.

An invitation to the déjeuner on Wednesday 15 October 1862 to mark the opening of the Hartley Institute. Reproduced by courtesy of Southampton Archives Services.

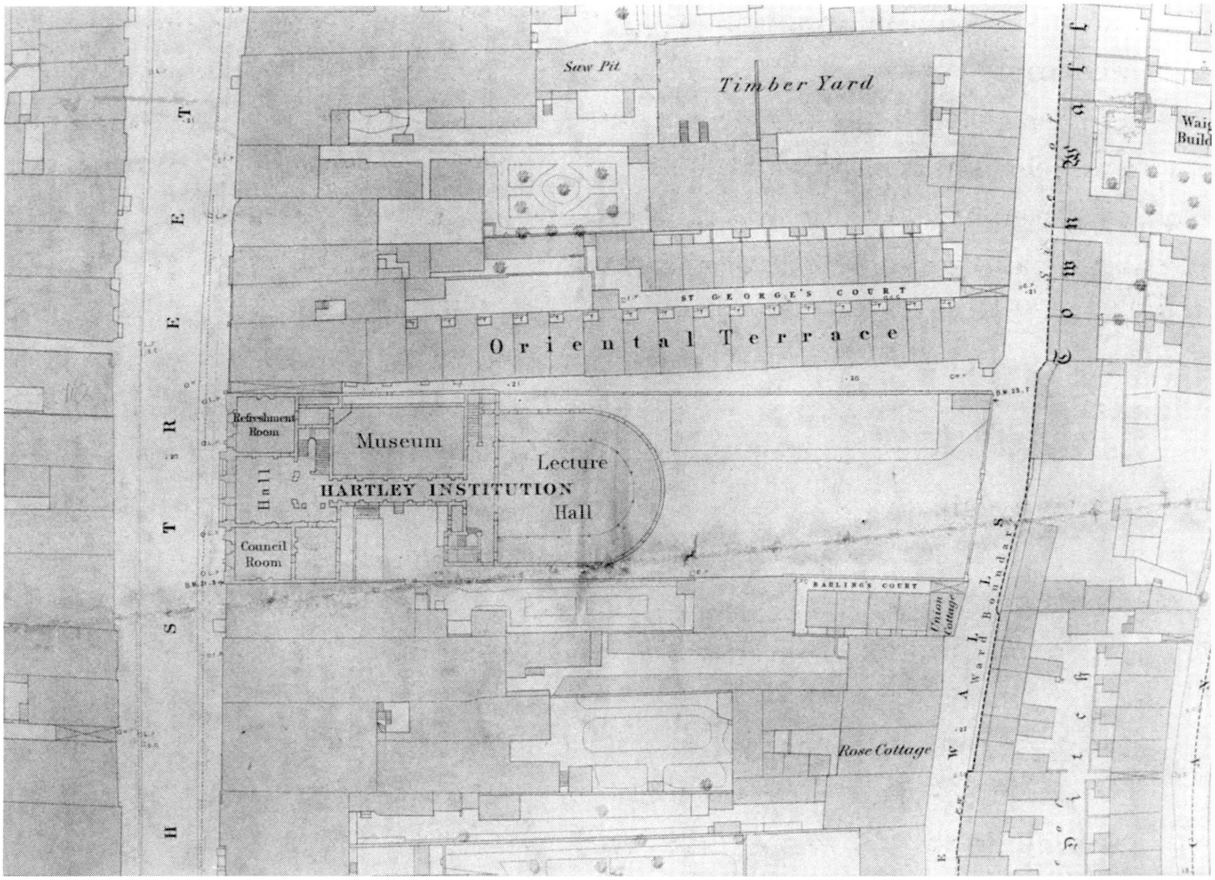

A PLAN OF THE HARTLEY INSTITUTE taken from a map of 1870. Note the curved shape of the Lecture Hall the interior of which is recorded in an engraving of the time. Reproduced by courtesy of the Ordnance Survey.

The Institution was opened in 1862, 12 years after Hartley's death, and the buildings were inaugurated officially by the Lord Viscount Palmerston. The event was marked by a *déjeuner* given by the Mayor of Southampton on Wednesday 15 October of that same year. The Institution remained as a seat of learning, until 1902 when this was recognised and its status was raised to that of a university college i.e. **Hartley University College**. As its activities increased the need arose to find a new site, and in response to this need a rural location in Highfield in the northern suburbs was chosen, to the east of Southampton Common. Although new buildings were completed on this site in 1914, they were not occupied or used until the end of the First World War. In a letter dated 10 September 1919, a Professor Eustice (then Professor of Engineering) writing to an intending student, said: 'the College is now transferring its main activities to the new site at Highfield. A few evening classes only will be held in the old engineering buildings at the Back of the Walls', and he goes on to say, 'during the War classes have been suspended owing to lack of qualified students'.

During the inter-war period, the University College expanded with some fine red brick buildings, particularly in the 1930s at the same time as Herbert Collins was busy building the Highfield Estates near to Christ Church in Highfield Lane. At the same time the Civic Centre in Southampton was likewise under construction to the designs of Berry Webber. It was not until 1952, however, that full university status was obtained, and at that time the expansion of the University site began in earnest, to an overall plan drawn up by the architects firm of Sir Basil Spence and Partners, on a site bounded to its west by Southampton Common and on the other sides by a typical suburban development of traditional villas, semi-detached and terraced housing.

The main building of the original 1930s complex is the **Hartley Library**, designed in 1935 by the local firm of Gutteridge & Gutteridge (now Gutteridges), in association with Sir Giles Gilbert Scott, no less. This is a very fine red brick edifice on two storeys beneath a Roman tiled roof. The tall, slender mullioned windows give the building a distinctly ecclesiastical air, and together with some particularly intricate detailing of the brickwork and leaded lights to the windows, set the scale and standard appropriate for a new seat of learning. This building is flanked by the earlier 1914 buildings by the architects firm of Mitchell, Son & Gutteridge, again some consummate brick detailing and colouring, and with some variation in style and design compared to the 1930s building, brought about by the use of stone for window mullions and arched entrances, as well as heavy rustications to the lower storey.

The University campus was then, as today, a seemingly amorphous area of land with no clearly defined edges, other than its western boundary with Southampton Common. Although there are apparently hard boundaries in the form of roads, these demarcations are breached by associated developments beyond. For instance, to the north there is the line of Burgess Road, past which we see the Glen Eyre and Chamberlain halls of residence, and the so-called Boldrewood Site housing the Biomedical Sciences Building, all set in beautifully landscaped settings inherited from fine old houses now demolished. To the east is Broadlands Road and Hartley Avenue, and to the south the University extends to just north of the junction of Welbeck Avenue and Church Lane, which leads directly to Highfield and, as the name suggests, to Highfield's parish church, Christ Church. The present Local Plan for Southampton states that the University's expansion policy shall be on the basis of 'a minimal loss of residential accommodation', i.e. the adjoining houses, although parts of the Highfield and Hampton Park suburbs are definitely in the shadow of the University, albeit not oppressively so. Certain local roads have, however, already been assimilated into the campus, for instance, Salisbury Road and University Crescent to the west and east of University Road respectively. The contemporary University is part of a conscious decision to allow the campus to develop as part of what is described as an 'urban solution', as opposed to the idea of moving outwards to a new greenfield site.

When in 1914 the initial campus building had been completed, a competition was held to produce plans for new buildings and a layout for the whole site. As a result, a London practice of Messrs Clyde Young and H.B. East were judged the best. But the hiatus of the war years and the need to improvise in the subsequent lean years, led to a seemingly *ad hoc* approach. As has already been stated, the newly completed buildings were not immediately occupied by the Hartley University College, for on 20 May 1914, having been formally opened by the Lord Chancellor, Lord Haldane, the premises were at once requisitioned by the War Department as a military hospital. Because of the need to keep pace with the number of casualties arriving from the battlefields of France, wooden huts were erected behind to act as emergency hospital wards, and it was these same temporary buildings which came into use by the College after the end of hostilities. Sir Sidney Kimber, who lived nearby in a property called 'Oakdene' in Welbeck Avenue, was involved in the administration of the new University College in his official capacity with the then Town Council. He wrote of the establishment's financial constraints in its formative years, which led to slow progress and a watering-down of the high ideals of the 1914 'master plan' drawn up by Clyde Young and H.B. East. Be that as it may, the development of the site continued during those inter-war years, coupled with a steady increase in the number of students.

Reference has already been made to the location and boundaries of the site, but it is interesting to discover the uses of the land which is now occupied by the current University buildings. Firstly on the west side of University Road (formerly known as Back Lane) in the southern-most section, was a brickworks owned by Sir Sidney Kimber. This site was overlooked to the north by a property called 'the

Green'. On the other side of the road, opposite the brickworks, was another property called Church Farm. Over the area of the old brickworks we now see the West Building, i.e. the Old Refectory (the Student Union), the Shackleton Building (formerly the Geology Department which has since moved to the new Southampton Oceanography building, and its wonderful Geological Museum, once the centrepiece of the Shackleton building, has now been dismantled) and the Physics Building, all set on undulating levels in part. The original stream runs through the site, with its water and associated lush vegetation. The Nuffield Theatre stands on part of the Green, bounded to the north by Salisbury Road, while on the other side of University Road we see the Bookshop Building where once stood Church Farm.

Local brickyards were a constant feature of the Hampshire economy in the 19th and early 20th centuries, as were small 'suburban' farmsteads, both, however, falling to decline and redevelopment as part of the contemporary theme of the time. The site in its entirety has been described as 'an oasis of green fields', a character which has been encapsulated in the landscape around Spence's Buildings of the 1960s, particularly on the West Site.

Certain buildings stand out for attention. Moving in an anti-clockwise motion from the north-west corner of the site, we can start with the strikingly bold **Mathematics and Computing Building** designed by Ronald Sims in 1965. It is essentially a ten-storey building comprising a three-storey brick-clad podium with a grand entrance storey above; an overhanging six-storey element completes the composition. The external appearance of the upper storeys is of reinforced concrete straight from the shutters, in a style first written about in the *Architectural Review* in the 1950s. It was described as the New Brutalism, although few of the architects of the day would admit to being 'brutalists'. It is nevertheless a very powerful *tour de force* and was once described by Pevsner Lloyd as being 'of striking and attractive shape'. It is a monochrome building from a monochrome age, but self-confident and assertive nevertheless, and typical of its time.

THE NUFFIELD THEATRE with a F. E. McWilliam sculpture in the foreground.

The **Nuffield Theatre** was begun in 1961, designed by Sir Basil Spence, Bonnington and Collins in conjunction with Dr Richard Southern. It is a low-slung building, almost without visible windows, with a powerful brick lower storey and inclined roofs in copper above the auditorium and stage area. The building is set around an attractive courtyard garden, incorporating pools and sculpture as a setting to the Law and Arts Building and Staff Club Building (both by Spence's firm). The orientation of this fine group on a north-east to south-west slant has been set in parallel in relation to the front facade of the Hartley Library on the opposite side of University Road, i.e. on the East Site. So began a geometrical relationship of the new buildings on the campus to the traditional buildings which existed at the time. This form of layout when extended was against the natural contours of the landscape, in a way described by the designers as 'the foil of the organic with the rectilinear', in other words the poetry of straight lines seen against the flowing forms of nature. This concept is very much in line with the 18th century concept of 'le Jardin Anglais' – undulating grassed areas leading to an irregularly-shaped water feature, over which a bridge arches, seen against more rigid building forms, such as we see in miniature in the centre of the West Site. It is this fusion of landscape and architectural form which is central to the design philosophy of the 1960s and makes the university campus quite outstanding.

The initial layout proposals for the modern University in Southampton were embodied in a report published in 1962 entitled 'Proposals for Development' to illustrate guidelines for development of the site over the following 20 years. Circulation-wise, this plan diverted the north-south line of University Road, dividing the East Site from the West Site, and allowed for the filtering of traffic through and around the edges of the campus, now broadly defined by Burgess Road to the north, the Common to the west, Highfield Lane to the south and Hartley Avenue to the east. It also included new teaching and residential blocks. The original site, purchased in 1910, with subsequent enlargements, amounted to 32 acres (12.95

THE STUDENTS' UNION BUILDING in its fine landscaped setting described by the designers as 'the foil of the organic with the rectilinear'; in other words, the poetry of straight lines seen against the flowing forms of nature

hectares), while the new plan envisaged an overall increase in the site to 54 acres (21.85 hectares) in total to allow for future expansion. Care and attention was given to ensure that, as far as practical, there was no infringement of daylighting on properties adjoining the campus, and to ensure also that the occupiers of properties which were to be assimilated into the scheme should bear the minimum inconvenience. At least that was the basis of the planning brief at that time. Each new

THE FARADAY BUILDING (with the Lanchester Building in the foreground).
"The most exciting building on the present campus"

project was overseen by both the Joint Development Committee and a Planning Committee, while each individual scheme was designed taking into account the end users' views, ensuring that most buildings were sited close to others, linked in function for ease of movement and the convenience of both staff and students.

As in life it is easy to invoke criticism when expressing personal choices, but one of the most exciting buildings on the present campus must be the Faraday Building linked to the Eustice Building and the Lanchester Building, all three being concerned with engineering. The **Faraday Building** is very much a quintessential 60s building: ten storeys in height, square in plan, with horizontal panels of glazing and mosaic panelling. The upper storeys are cantilevered out from their podium. Seen from a distance at night with its illuminated windows glowing, it makes a dramatic sight indeed. Today there is great need for the enhancement and preservation of these fine 1960s buildings on the campus, notwithstanding the maintenance problems which abound. This form of architecture was born of a particular era in our society, during a period of great sociological change, not least of which was the desire to extend universally the chance of a higher education which was no longer limited to the privileged few. It is therefore up to succeeding generations to build on these new advantages, and to ensure that the new environment of the campus is nurtured, and its buildings and landscape, designed by architects with an international reputation, be protected and preserved for posterity.

HOUSE AT
LINGWOOD CLO
BASSETT
Architects:
Peter Kilby Associat
P. Kilby FRIBA,
W. Miadowicz
Practice Secretary:
E. Diaper
Engineers:
G.KN Reinforcemen

This house, designed for Mr and Mrs A. Samuels in 1968, is now owned by Mr and Mrs P. Turner who kindly consented to the inclusion of these photographs.

EXTERIOR
from Lingwood Close.

INTERIOR
The first floor south facing living rooms.

11. MODERN SOUTHAMPTON

THE 1950S

When Queen Elizabeth II succeeded her father King George VI to the throne in 1953, so began a new period in our history which was to be reflected not only in the environment but also in the way we were to live. Behind us all were the dark days of austerity and a new age was heralded through the symbolism of the conquest of the 29,028 feet (8847.73 metres) summit of Mount Everest by Sir Edmund Hilary and Sherpa Tensing, the news of which reached this country on the day of the Coronation.

In Southampton a year earlier in 1952, a bold new plan had been published setting out a blueprint for the future reconstruction of the city, like the phoenix rising from the ashes of war. The aim of the plan was set out as follows: '... to make the best and fullest use of the available area and to provide as far as possible for ... the proper functioning of shopping and the commercial centre of the town and the surrounding area'. In order to make it possible for the plan to be put into effect, a so-called 'Declaratory Order' was made under the 1944 Town and Country Planning Act 'by which it is declared to be the subject of a compulsory purchase order by the Council ... for the purpose of dealing with extensive war damage.' This order extended to an area of some 272 acres (110.07 hectares) of the city centre.

So the stage was set for the reconstruction programme to commence, providing at the same time the opportunity to alter the pattern of land uses, to assimilate new roads and to rationalise the zoning of activities. Initially a five-year plan was adopted by the Borough as a whole to concentrate on the broad areas of Above Bar, the High Street, East Street, London Road, Hoglands housing area and the Central Station, at an estimated total cost of £6.3 million. A great deal of painstaking research

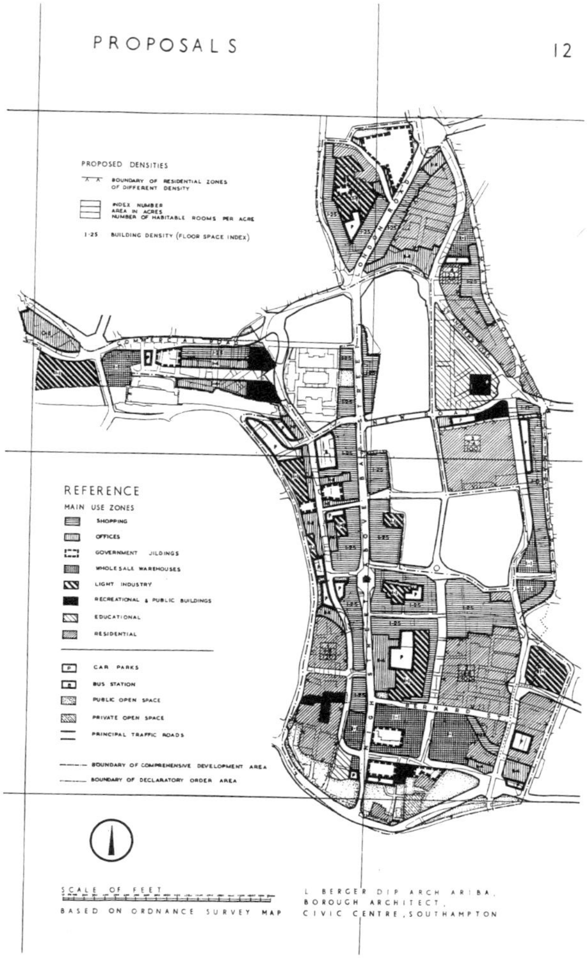

1952 PLAN FOR SOUTHAMPTON
(Copy of plan held by Southampton Archives Services) 'A bold new plan ... a blueprint for the future reconstruction of the city'.
(By courtesy of Ordnance Survey and Southampton Archives Services)

had gone into the plan, with an analytical and systematic approach. However it barely touched on design issues in the third dimension (i.e. as opposed to layout plans), and at best was an instrument to get things moving in an orderly way, to build on war-damaged sites and to re-house the business and domestic users, some of whom were in temporary buildings, into new purpose-built premises.

In contrast to this approach another plan had been produced ten years earlier in 1942 by Messrs Cook and Adshead. This was an independent planning report presented to Southampton Council, in which the initial research and findings had gone further with suggested design solutions for various elements of the plan, together with some 'broad brush' proposals for the central area. This plan was most imaginative in its approach and format and was said to be 'the first of its kind produced in this country'.

Of the town centre the consultants said 'unlike most towns those origins

SOUTHAMPTON: THE NEW CIVIC CENTRE
This is the title of Berry Webber's designs for the civic offices which go beyond the building itself and show how the surroundings could be developed to create the 'central space or square' referred to in the later 1942 plans for the city centre prepared by Messrs. Cook and Professor Adshead. Reproduced by courtesy of Berry Webber and Partners (incorporated with AHP Partnership 1.1.96) and taken from a photograph held in the Southampton Archives Services.

date back to Medieval times, Southampton has no central square or place.' With this in mind, it was suggested that the newly constructed Civic Centre should form the focus of such a place, with the Guildhall forming the 'dominant feature'. This is very much in line with the thinking of the Civic Centre's architect Berry Webber, for in his perspective drawing of his winning design he demonstrates in the background a monumental group of buildings forming a fine piazza or square. Further in the background are the parks; what a wonderful place this would have been if imagination had become a reality! Other proposals included grand designs for the waterfront with a new 'pavilion and pier for the Isle of Wight steamers', and a large area of open space between the water and what is now the Western Esplanade to act as a 'site for an exhibition'. This vast area was to stretch from the pier to the Central Station.

In the introduction to their report, Cook and Adshead say 'Southampton's reconstruction should be something more than the repair of damage following a catastrophe by enemy action ... this occasion, however, is one which calls for something more than merely rebuilding, it having occurred in a period in the history of Southampton when very important changes were being called for in social conditions in the housing of people and in transport' – this quotation says it all!

THE 1960S

In spite of misconceptions to the contrary, the 1960s were years of some great achievements, for public morale at least. On 17 July 1964, Donald Campbell broke the world land speed record in his car *Bluebird II* with a speed of 403.135 m.p.h. on the salt flats at Lake Eyre in Australia. The new motoring public were introduced to the Austin and Morris mini cars, the brainchild of Sir Alec Issigonis. On 20 September 1967, the liner *Queen Elizabeth II* was launched, and after sea trials, sailed on her maiden voyage from Southampton to New York on 2 May 1969. Concorde, now with its four Rolls-Royce/Snecma Olympus 593 engines, first flew supersonic on 1 October 1969 prior to eventually achieving MACH 2 or 1350 m.p.h. on 4 November 1970. It was in many ways a new era of transportation which was to change the lives and aspirations of its people.

The most significant buildings of the 1960s in Southampton (apart from the Eric Lyons flats of Castle House in Castle Way) are those at the University campus. However, at South Stoneham House (a University hall of residence site within the Itchen Valley Conservation Area and a space of considerable natural beauty in the

many people standing on interior escalators, or in the scenic life, the cosy womb-like basement food halls, the internal planting (usually artificial) and background music to mask most human sounds, all contributed to a seemingly surreal atmosphere.

The psychology behind all this was to induce people to spend money without feeling guilty!

THE BARGATE CENTRE

Inside the old town walls, in the north-east corner, such a shopping centre has been planned , on a site once occupied by a large brewery called the 'Bottlery'. It was an awkward, land-locked site with no easy access, bisected by a road running north-south called York Buildings. The idea of the developers was to provide a large shopping centre in this space and to form pedestrian links with the Bargate

THE BARGATE CENTRE
This was designed by W.H. Saunders and Son. There is a splendid drumlike feature marking the southern entrance from East Street.
Photograph by Peter Kilby.

itself. At the north of York Buildings was the site of the York Gate which had previously been lost, but the remainder of the old town wall to the north was still left standing and stretched from near the Bargate eastwards towards Polymond Tower. There were two old buildings left on the site, Nos 1 and 2 York Buildings, one of which was reputed to have been the one-time residence of T.E. Lawrence, i.e. Lawrence of Arabia. In many respects the building which has evolved is very much inward-looking and non-elevational, other than the south approach from East Street, where there is a splendid drum-like feature in brickwork flanking to the left of the glazed entrance at the lowest level. Inside the interior is one of considerable restraint, designed by Fitch & Co. in collaboration with the architects W.H. Saunders & Son, with terrazzo floors to the sloping malls, so constructed as to deal with cross levels on the site. There is a large open space where the centre of the road, York Buildings, once was and to the north of this are replica reproductions of the two town houses demolished during the construction and formulative design. This is an example of a large shopping complex which has in many ways been successfully integrated within the historic fabric of the old town, in spite of the loss of the original Nos 1 and 2 York Buildings.

OCEAN VILLAGE

On the waterfront in the vicinity of the Princess Alexandra Dock, in the Old Docks, and Canute Road stands Ocean Village. Designed by Manchester architects Covell, Matthews and Histon and opened in 1986, it is an example of an ambitious mixed development on land owned by Associated British Ports. Carried out without grants from central government, the principal feature is a two-level shopping complex, with ancillary facilities called 'Canute's Pavilion', partly new and in part integrating some of the original dock buildings. These buildings are grouped around a 450 berth marina within the Princess Alexandra Dock itself. Canute's Pavilion has a lightweight, transitory feel about its architecture, using brightly-coloured materials

OCEAN VILLAGE
Opened in 1986 and built around the Princess Alexandra Dock it forms a splendid setting for viewing the marina and ocean-going yachts and pleasure craft.

and a maritime image of impending movement. The building itself plays host to many activities with shops, bars, restaurants and some offices, all on two levels, although it is fair to say that the units on the ground floor fare better than those above. The best thing about this building is the view it affords from inside of the marina outside, with its yachts and pleasure craft of all shapes and sizes, while a flock of swans glide serenely over the water, having made the marina their home.

THE 1990S

Without doubt the major event of this decade is the planning and emergence of the Esplanade Development over an area of 35 acres (14.16 hectares) of reclaimed land. This scheme, designed by the Building Design Partnership, will eventually encompass some 53 acres (21.44 hectares) of development on a site defined to the east by the Western Esplanade and to the west by West Quay Road, while forging links with Above Bar itself, crossing the Western Esplanade and Portland Terrace in the process. The area so defined is similar to the open space in the Cook and Adshead plan of 1942 but there the similarity ends. The scale of the plan is such that it must move the centre of gravity of the town centre away from the historic north-south axis of Above Bar and the High Street. Great care needs to be exercised where this development comes in close contact with the north-west corner of the medieval town walls, particularly when considering the question of relative scale. It is a bold plan and only time will tell whether it will be achieved with finesse.

Standing on top of the Arundel Tower on the old town walls, overlooking the Pirelli site with distant views of the New Docks, it is interesting to muse on how J.B. Priestley would have reacted to the new scene, 60 years on from his *English Journey.* He talked of the visiting liners and of 'building a town, and planning a life worthy of such majestic company – what a Southampton that would be'.

EPILOGUE

In Chapter 7, the unknown writer of 1919 describes the difficulty of grasping the form of Southampton, other than from the 'Navigation Bridge of a great Atlantic liner, and the other from the vantage point of the Itchen at Peartree Green.' Today, however, regular flights from the Channel Islands provide a progressive and grandstand view from the air of the city, approaching from say the South-West, above the Isle of Wight Needles. Firstly there is the Solent where, as the Venerable Bede stated 'in this narrow sea the two tides of the Ocean meet', generating the dual tides of the port. To the left is the River Test, with the vast refinery of Fawley backdropped by the lush green of the New Forest, while to the right the River Itchen meanders its way to the north, with bridges crossing from side to side, the one at Northam marking the site of Clausentum at Bitterne on the unmistakable peninsula where the Roman encampment once stood. Centre stage we pass over the Old Docks and Ocean Village, and on the left the New Docks stretching to the horizon, with the Redbridge Causeway and the Furlongs nature reserve beyond. Between the two rivers is the site of the medieval walled town (hard against the waterfront in early Victorian times), and just to the right again the spire of St Mary's Church marks the place where once stood the Saxon town and port of Hamwic on the Itchen.

The flight path to Southampton Airport then runs parallel with the general flow of the Itchen above the remainder of the 'modern' city, until we see the Ford Motor Company works and the M27 snaking eastwards to Portsmouth, the aircraft having just passed over the beautiful water meadows and old salmon pond around Woodmill. The shadow of the aircraft travels over the ground below until the runway at Southampton Eastleigh Airport comes into immediate view. We see the fine new terminal buildings designed by Michael Manser for the British Airport Authority, the sweeping curves of the roofs and metallic surfaces reminiscent of the aircraft which the building has been designed to serve. At touchdown the modern appearance of the new surroundings belies the history once enacted on these runways with the first flight of the Supermarine Spitfire prototype in the 1930s.

So ends the story of a city constantly changing like the moods of the seasons, the shades of night and the sunlight of the day. Southampton is dominated by its natural landscape features, the power of the waterfronts and the softness of the trees and grassed spaces. The man-made environment intervenes with varying measures of success and longevity. However, the words of Le Corbusier, that giant among 20th century architects, seem appropriate here 'you employ stone, wood and concrete, and with these materials you build houses and palaces, that is construction ingenuity at work. But suddenly you touch my heart and I say that is beautiful. That is architecture, when arts enters in'.

SOUTHAMPTON INTERNATIONAL AIRPORT
Architects Manser Associates
Photograph by kind permission of Michael Manser

BBC BUILDING Opposite the Civic Centre
A modern building with a respect both for its setting and traditional values of good manners (architecturally speaking)

BIBLIOGRAPHY

BOOKS

Austin-Leigh, R.A. *Jane Austen and Southampton*, London, Spottiswoode Ballantyne and Co. Ltd, 1949

Bede. *Ecclesiastical History of the English People*, London, Penguin Books, 1990

Biddle, G. and Nock, O.S. *The Railway Heritage of Britain*, London, Sheldrake Press Ltd, 1983

Brannon, P. *Picture of Southampton*, 1850, Republished Alresford, Lawrence Oxley, 1973

Cotton, M.A. and Gathercole, P.W. *Excavations at Clausentum Southampton,* London, HMSO, 1958

Domesday Survey - Hampshire, London and Manchester, Philmore & Co. Ltd, 1982

Douch, R. *Monuments and Memorials in Southampton*, 2nd edition, City of Southampton, 1978

Duthy, J. *Sketches of Hampshire*, 1830, Republished Alresford, Lawrence Oxley, 1972

Edgar Mann, J. *Southampton People*, Southampton, Ensign Publications, 1989

Englefield, Sir H.C. *A Walk Through Southampton,* London, Printed for T. Baker, 1841

Hardingham, R. (Ed.) *150 Years of L.S.W.R.*, Southampton and Reading, Kingfisher Railway Publications, 1988

Heritage of Britain, London, Reader's Digest Association Ltd, 1976

Historic Buildings of Southampton, Southampton Museums Publications, 1957

Hodgson, J. *Southampton Castle*, City Museums Archaeology Series, Horndean, Milestone Publications

Holland, A.J. *Ships of British Oak*, David & Charles, 1971

Hooker, J. *Solent Shore*, Manchester, Carcanet New Press Limited, 1980

John, Second Lord Montague of Beaulieu, *Bucklers Hard and its Ships*, London, 1909

Le Corbusier *Towards a New Architecture*, London, The Architectural Press, 1970

Leonard, A.G.K. *Saving of Tudor House,* Southampton, Paul Cave Publications Ltd, 1987

McCart, N. *Atlantic Liners of the Cunard Line,* Wellingborough, Patrick Stephens Limited, 1990

Moody, B. *150 Years of Southampton Docks,* Southampton, Kingfisher Railway Publications, 1988

Morton, A.D. (Ed.) CBA Research Report No. 84 *Excavations at Hamwic*, Vol. 1, London, Council for British Archaeology, 1992

O'Dell, N. *The River Itchen* and *The River Test*, Southampton, Paul Cave Publications, 1979

Pay, S. *Hamwic: Southampton's Saxon Town,* Horndean, Milestone Publications, 1987

Pevsner, N. and Lloyd, D. *Hampshire and the Isle of Wight*, Harmondsworth, Penguin Books, 1967

Platt, C. *Medieval Southampton*, London and Boston, Routledge & Paul Kegan, 1973

Platt, C. *Archaeology in Medieval Southampton*, Southampton Museums and Art Gallery, 1976

Platt, C. and Coleman Smith, R. *Excavations in Medieval Southampton*, Vol. 1, Leicester University Press, 1975

Pugh, T.B. *Henry V and the Southampton Plot,* Southampton Record Series, Southampton University Press, 1988

Seymour, W.A., (Ed.) *A History of the Ordnance Survey,* Folkstone, W.M. Dawson & Sons Ltd, 1980

Shakespeare, W. *King Henry V*, Cambridge, The University Press, 1968

Silvester Davies, Rev. J. *A History of Southampton*, Gilbert & Co, Hamilton, Southampton and London, Adams & Co., 1883

Speed, Dr J. *History and Antiquity of Southampton*, 1770, Southampton, Reprinted by Cox & Sharland, 1909

Temple Patterson, A. *A History of Southampton, Vol. 1* (1700-1835), Southampton, Southampton University Press, 1966

The House of Elliots, Southampton, Publication Elliot Bros Ltd, 1992

The Southampton Guide, 1781, Third Edition, Southampton and London

The Southampton Guide, 1795, Fifth Edition, Southampton and London

Varley, T. *Hampshire*, Second Edition, London, A.C. Black Ltd, 1926

Warner, Rev. R. *An Attempt to Ascertain the Situation of Clausentum,* London, R. Blamire, 1792

Welch, E. *The Bankrupt Canal Southampton and Salisbury 1795-1808*, Southampton, City of Southampton, 1966

Williams, R. *Herbert Collins 1885-1975,* Paul Cave Publications Ltd, 1985

Wood, M. *Doomesday. A Search for the Roots of England,* BBC Books, 1986

NEWSPAPER ARTICLES AND JOURNALS

Architects Journal Centenary Issue, London, Emac Architecture, 1995

Bourdillon, J. *Southampton Anglo-Saxon Town Life and Animal Husbandry*

Brisbane, M. *Saxon Remains Uncovered*, Now in Southampton, December 1983

Clarke, T.A. *General Roy's Cannon Returns to Base,* Department of Engineering, Heathrow Airport

Consecration of St Peter's Church and the Borough Cemetery, The Hampshire Advertiser, 9-5-46

Corps, D.E. *The Story of Jesus Chapel (commonly called Pear Tree Church),* Southampton

Cottingham, E. *The Brickyards at Bailey's Hard (Countryside Education Trust, Beaulieu)*

Crossing the Itchen, The Southampton Corporation

First Example of Town Planning - The Polygon, Hampshire Advertiser, 16-1-37

Friends See Two Old Hotels, Southampton Daily Echo, 18-8-54

Hadrians Wall Official Guide, English Heritage
Hampshire Advertiser, 1940
Hampshire Field Club Archaeological Society Publication 36, 1980
Hartley on its Opening Day, The Hampshire Advertiser and the Southampton Times, 11-4-36
Itchen Bridge, City of Southampton
Hodges, R. *The 8th Century Pottery Industry at La Londe*, Antiquity 65, 1991
Holdsworth, P. *Report of Southampton Archaeological Committee*, Hamwic, Six Dials Excavations
Jones, S. *Tudor House,* (pamphlet) Southampton City Museums 1989
Leonard, A.C.K *Redbridge Shipbuilding,* Southern Evening Echo, 18-10-85
Lord Lieutenant Opens Northam Bridge, Southern Evening Echo, 20-10-54
McKenna, A. *Hamwic: Streets Ahead of the Rest*, Southern Evening Echo, 11-11-81
McKenna A. *We'll Rewrite Saxon History*, Southern Evening Echo, April 1980
McNaghten, A. I. *Bitterne Manor House* Official Architect and Planning 1953
New Light is Thrown on Old Clausentum, Southern Daily Echo, 25-6-51
Proposed New Pier for Southampton, Hampshire Independent, c.1890
Radford, Commander J. *The New Passenger Terminal at Southampton Docks*, Illustrated London News, 1950
Relics of Hamwic, View in Southampton, Spring 1984
Sandell, E. *Dep. Southampton 8.50 Arr. Waterloo 11.00 - Not bad for 1859*, Southern Daily Echo 26-6-88
Site of Clausentum Explored, Southern Daily Echo, 15-5-50
Stevens Curl, J. *Southampton Cemetery*, Hampshire County Magazine, 1984
Southampton Star Inn's Flashback to 1831, Southampton Daily Echo, 6-5-53
Southampton Reborn, A Daily Echo Publication, 28-1-95
St Marys South Stoneham Guide, Church Guide
The Facts of Saxon Life, Southern Evening Echo, 11-11-81
The Old Empire to be Demolished, Hampshire Advertiser, 27-1-40
Tilley, A. *Clausentum*, Southern Evening Echo, 20-9-91
Town Planning? They were doing it 1000 years ago, Now in Southampton, April 1980
Townsman *Coming of the Railway*, Southern Daily Echo 1-12-79
Townsman *Southampton to Dorchester Line*, Southern Daily Echo, 15-12-79
Randall Philips, R. *Townhill Park I*, Country Life, 14-4-23
Randall Philips, R. *Townhill Park II*, Country Life, 21-4-23

Waterman, D.M. *Antiquities Journal,* 1947

Wyeth Gadd, E. *Wessex Heritage' When great-grandpa took a trip by train,* Southern Daily Echo 10-7-82

White K. *St Mary's Church and Churchyard* Southampton City Council, 1994

Woodmill Salmon Fisheries, Southern Evening Echo, 7-8-89

RECORDS

City of Southampton Planning and Development Services (Records)

Gardiner, N. *The University of Southampton,* 1983

Regal Cinema, *Souvenir of opening,* June 1934

Southampton Archives Services, *1834 Act For Making a Railway from London to Southampton*

Southampton Archives Services, *Berry Webber's Competition Drawings and Contract Documentation*

Southampton Archives Services, *Southampton in 1620 and the Mayflower,* 1970

Southampton Archives Services, *Souvenir Programme of the opening of the Municipal Block*

Southampton, London and Branch Railway and Dock Company Prospectus, 1831

The Register of Historic Parks and Gardens of Special Historical Interest in England The Central Parks Southampton (Statistics), Associated British Ports

University of Southampton, *Hartley Library Special Collections*

University of Southampton, *Proposals for Development,* Southampton University Press, 1962

W.H. Saunders and Son, *Bargate Centre Tenant Manual*

Hampshire County Library, Special Collections, Civic Centre, Southampton

DISPLAYS

God's House Tower Archaeology Museum

Hall of Aviation

The Buildings of Bath Museum

Tudor House Museum

MAPS/PLANS

Berger, L. *1952 Plan,* Southampton Archives Services

Cook and Adshead *1942 Plan,* Southampton Archives Services

Geo Doswell Map, 1842

Illustrative Masterplan of the Esplanade Development July 1995, Southampton, Southampton City Council and Imry Ltd.

Map of Roman Britain, 3rd Edition, Published by Ordnance Survey, 1956

Map 1851 John Tallis & Co. Ltd.

Map 1978 British Transport Docks Board

Southampton Maps, published by Southampton Corporation, 1964:

Elizabethan Southampton (1)

Speed *Southampton in 1611* (3)

Mazell *Southampton in 1771 (8)*

Southampton in 1791 (11)

Southampton in 1800 (13)

Southampton in 1802 (15)

Southampton in 1835 (19)

War Damage in Southampton, 1939-45 (24)

Ordnance Survey Maps 1845-6 3 No. maps, Southampton Archives Services

Visitors Map of University Building Numbers, University of Southampton

THANKS ARE DUE TO JOE LOW FOR THE USE OF THE FOLLOWING PHOTOGRAPHS WHICH APPEAR IN THIS BOOK.

INSIDE BACK COVER

PETER KILBY

PROLOGUE

MADONNA FIGURE FROM ST DENYS CHURCH

1. HISTORICAL INTRODUCTIONS

PLAN OF CLAUSENTUM; BATH HOUSE; ROMAN STATION; BATH HOUSE FOUNDATIONS; THE DEFENSIVE "FOSSE"; BITTERNE MANOR TODAY

2. THE MEDIEVAL WALLED TOWN AND TOWN QUAYS

SHIELDS; BARGATE (North Side); SENTINEL LIONS; NEW BELL OR WATCH BELL; BARGATE (South Side); CASTLE EAST GATE; CASTLE WATERGATE; CASTLE WEST GATE; BULLS HEAD INN; ST. JULIENS CHAPEL; THE EAST WINDOWS OF THE CHAPEL; THE VAULTS

3. THE GOLDEN AGE OF SPA AND THE RESORT PERIOD

STAR HOTEL; ELEGANT LAMPPOST OUTSIDE THE COURTYARD ENTRANCE TO THE DOLPHIN; DOLPHIN HOTEL

4. SOUTHAMPTON DOCKS - THE OLD AND NEW

MAP OF 1870; MURAL; GOODS AND ENGINE SHED; FERRY HOUSE; CANUTE CHAMBERS; DART HOUSE; DART HOUSE (A DETAIL OF THE PEDIMENT); WILTS & DORSET BANK; UNION CASTLE HOUSE; TRAFALGAR DRY DOCK; WINDWARD TERMINAL; KING GEORGE V GRAVING DOCK

5. THE LONDON AND SOUTHWESTERN RAILWAY AND ILL-FATED CANAL

MAP OF 1870; RAILWAY TIMETABLE; TERMINUS STATION; ST. DENYS STATION; ORNATE BRIDGE AT ST. DENYS STATION

6. THE VICTORIAN ERA

PLAQUE AT ORDNANCE SURVEY BUILDING; WESTERN RANGE OF OFFICES; 125 HIGH STREET (HOLY ROOD CHAMBERS); SOUTH WESTERN HOUSE; ROYAL SOUTH HANTS HOSPITAL; CHRIST CHURCH HIGHFIELD; ST DENYS CHURCH STONEWORK; ST DENYS CHURCH STONEWORK; HOLY SAVIOUR CHURCH, BITTERNE; ST JAMES, SHIRLEY

7. OPEN SPACES

CARVED STONE MASK; SOUTHAMPTON COMMON CEMETERY; GRAVES AND CHAPEL; STATUE OF ISAAC WATTS IN WATTS PARK; COBDEN BRIDGE; MANSBRIDGE

8. THE INTERWAR YEARS

BERRY WEBBERS ORIGINAL COMPETITION WINNING DESIGNS FOR THE CIVIC CENTRE (1928); MAYOR'S RECEPTION ROOM; MAYORS CORRIDOR/SUITE; HERBERT COLLINS PLAQUE; A PORTMEIRION SETTING; ORCHARDS WAY; UPLANDS ESTATE; GLEBE COURT; THE ODEON CINEMA

9. WORLD WAR II

THE SUPERMARINE SPITFIRE

10. THE UNIVERSITY OF SOUTHAMPTON AND THE HARTLEY INSTITUTION

HARTLEY ENGRAVING; INVITATION TO THE DEJEUNER; PLAN OF THE HARTLEY INSTITUTE; THE NUFFIELD THEATRE; THE STUDENTS' UNION BUILDING; THE FARADAY BUILDING

11. MODERN SOUTHAMPTON

INTERIOR OF HOUSE AT LINGWOOD CLOSE, BASSETT; EXTERIOR OF HOUSE; SOUTHAMPTON: THE NEW CIVIC CENTRE; THE BARGATE CENTRE; OCEAN VILLAGE

12. EPILOGUE

BBC BUILDING

INDEX

T